Algorithmic Trading: Navigating the Future of Finance

Alex Thompson

Published by Side Hustle Success, 2023.

ALGORITHMIC TRADING: NAVIGATING THE FUTURE OF FINANCE

First edition. October 3, 2023.

ISBN: 979-8223424499

Written by Alex Thompson.

Also by Alex Thompson

Alex on Finance

Financial Freedom Roadmap - Achieving Early Retirement through the FIRE Movement

The Art of Strategic Innovation

Beyond Cash - The Evolution of Digital Payment Systems and the Future of Money

Preserving Wealth in Inflationary Times - Strategies for Protecting Your Financial Future

Standalone

Side Hustle Success: Unlocking Your Entrepreneurial Potential

Side Hustle Success: The Ultimate Guide to Passive and Financial Freedom

Mastering the Markets: Advanced Trading Strategies for Success and Ethical Trading Practices

Financial Fortitude

Mastering the Art of Upselling

The Financial Bullet Blueprint

Investing Demystified: A Beginner's Guide to Building Wealth in the Stock Market

Real Estate Riches: Building Wealth through Property Investment

How To Succeed as a Freelancer

Navigating Complex Waters: Advanced Strategies in Portfolio Management
Behavioral Finance and Investor Psychology
Leading with Empathy: Harnessing Emotional Intelligence for Effective Leadership
Financial Independence
Thriving Within Your Means: A Guide to Affordable Living
Algorithmic Trading: Navigating the Digital Frontier
Navigating Alternative Investments
Navigating the Behavioral Finance Landscape
Unlocking the Power of Derivatives
Mastering International Finance
Quantitative Finance and Risk Modeling
Sustainable and ESG Investing
Derivatives Dynamics: Navigating Risk and Innovation
Options Mastery: Navigating the Financial Frontier
Portfolio Mastery: Navigating the Financial Art and Science
Ethics in Hedge Funds: Navigating the Moral Compass of Finance
Structured Finance: Navigating Innovation, Sustainability and Ethics
Commodity Trading: Navigating Markets, Sustainability, and Innovation
Ethical Valuation: Navigating the Future of Startup Investments
Navigating Financial Risk: Strategies for a Dynamic World
Navigating the New Frontier: Understanding Market Microstructure in the Digital Age
Mastering Mergers and Acquisitions: Strategies, Successes and Lessons
Mastering Real Estate Investment: Strategies, Trends and Success Stories
Navigating Investor Behavior: Insights from Behavioral Finance
Private Equity Horizons: Navigating Opportunities and Shaping the Future
Algorithmic Trading: Navigating the Future of Finance

To those who navigate the complexities of financial markets with unwavering dedication, innovation, and integrity, and to the bright minds shaping the future of algorithmic trading.

Chapter 1: Introduction to Algorithmic Trading

What Is Algorithmic Trading?

Algorithmic trading, often referred to as algo trading, is a sophisticated method of trading financial assets such as stocks, bonds, currencies, commodities, and derivatives using computer algorithms. These algorithms are designed to execute a predefined set of trading strategies automatically, without human intervention, at a speed and frequency that is impossible for a human trader to achieve manually.

Key characteristics and components of algorithmic trading include:

1. **Algorithm Development:** Traders or quantitative analysts (quants) create algorithms that specify the conditions under which trades should be executed. These algorithms can range from simple rules-based strategies to complex mathematical models.

2. **Automated Execution:** Once an algorithm is developed, it is programmed into a computer system. This system continuously monitors financial markets, analyzes data, and executes trades based on the algorithm's instructions. This automation allows for rapid execution and minimizes the impact of human emotions on trading decisions.

3. **High-Speed Trading:** Algorithmic trading systems operate at incredibly high speeds, often executing trades in milliseconds or microseconds. This speed advantage can be crucial when attempting to exploit short-lived market inefficiencies or arbitrage opportunities.

4. **Quantitative Analysis:** Algorithmic trading relies heavily on quantitative analysis and statistical modeling. Traders use historical

data and mathematical techniques to optimize their algorithms and assess their performance.

5. **Risk Management:** Effective risk management is critical in algorithmic trading. Algorithms are designed to manage risk by setting predefined stop-loss levels, position-sizing rules, and other risk controls to protect capital.

6. **Market Connectivity:** Algorithmic traders need fast and reliable connectivity to financial markets. They often use specialized trading platforms and co-location services to reduce latency and execute orders as quickly as possible.

7. **Market Liquidity:** Algorithmic traders often focus on liquid markets where there is a high volume of trading activity. Liquidity allows for the efficient execution of large orders without significantly impacting the market price.

8. **Trading Strategies:** Algorithmic trading encompasses a wide range of trading strategies, including market making, statistical arbitrage, trend following, and more. The choice of strategy depends on the trader's goals and risk tolerance.

9. **Regulatory Compliance:** Algorithmic trading is subject to regulatory oversight to ensure fair and orderly markets. Traders must comply with rules and regulations set by financial authorities, including circuit breaker mechanisms to prevent excessive market volatility.

Algorithmic trading has become increasingly popular in financial markets due to its ability to execute trades with precision, speed, and efficiency. It is widely used by institutional investors, hedge funds, proprietary trading firms, and even some retail traders who have access to algorithmic trading platforms.

However, it is important to note that algorithmic trading also comes with risks, such as technical glitches, market disruptions, and the potential for unintended consequences. Therefore, traders and firms engaging in algorithmic trading must have robust risk management practices and infrastructure in place.

The Evolution of Algorithmic Trading

Algorithmic trading has undergone significant evolution since its inception. Here is a brief overview of its key milestones and developments:

1. **Early Beginnings (1980s):** The origins of algorithmic trading can be traced back to the 1980s when financial firms started using computer programs to automate trading tasks. Initially, these systems were relatively simple and focused on executing orders efficiently.

2. **The Rise of Electronic Exchanges (1990s):** The 1990s saw the emergence of electronic exchanges and the gradual shift away from traditional open outcry trading floors. Electronic trading platforms provided the foundation for algorithmic trading to thrive, as they offered faster execution and better transparency.

3. **Decimalization (2001):** In the early 2000s, many stock exchanges in the United States switched from fractional pricing to decimal pricing, which increased the complexity of trading. Algorithmic trading became essential for handling orders in this new environment.

4. **Regulatory Changes (2000s):** Regulatory changes, such as the Regulation NMS (National Market System) in the U.S., aimed to improve market access and transparency. These changes encouraged the development of new trading technologies, including algorithmic trading systems.

5. **High-Frequency Trading (HFT) (Mid-2000s):** High-frequency trading, a subset of algorithmic trading, gained prominence in the mid-2000s. HFT firms use extremely fast algorithms to execute a large number of trades in fractions of a second, often capitalizing on minuscule price differentials. This approach sparked debates about market stability and fairness.

6. **Quantitative Revolution (2000s):** Quantitative trading, driven by mathematicians and statisticians (quants), gained popularity. These traders developed complex mathematical models and algorithms to identify trading opportunities and manage risk.

7. **Global Expansion (2000s):** Algorithmic trading expanded globally, reaching markets beyond the United States. It became prevalent in European, Asian, and other international financial markets.

8. **Flash Crash (2010):** The May 6, 2010, Flash Crash, during which the U.S. stock market experienced a rapid and severe drop followed by a swift recovery, raised concerns about the impact of algorithmic and high-frequency trading on market stability. It prompted discussions on circuit breakers and market safeguards.

9. **Market Microstructure Innovations (2010s):** Exchanges and regulatory authorities introduced new market microstructure innovations to address the challenges posed by algorithmic trading. These included mechanisms to prevent excessive volatility and limit erroneous trades.

10. **Machine Learning and AI (2010s):** In the latter part of the 2010s, machine learning and artificial intelligence (AI) technologies started to play a more prominent role in algorithmic trading. These technologies were used to develop more adaptive and data-driven trading strategies.

11. **Retail Algorithmic Trading (2010s):** With the advancement of technology, retail traders gained access to algorithmic trading

platforms, allowing them to automate their trading strategies. This democratization of algorithmic trading opened up new opportunities for individual investors.

12. **Regulatory Scrutiny (Ongoing):** Algorithmic trading continues to be subject to regulatory scrutiny worldwide. Authorities are working to strike a balance between encouraging innovation and ensuring market stability and fairness.

The evolution of algorithmic trading reflects the broader trend of technology's increasing role in financial markets. As technology continues to advance, algorithmic trading will likely continue to evolve, incorporating new tools and strategies to navigate an ever-changing financial landscape.

The role of algorithms in modern financial markets is significant and multifaceted. Algorithms have transformed how trading is conducted, providing numerous benefits and challenges. Here are some key roles and aspects of algorithms in modern markets:

1. **Efficiency:** Algorithms are designed to execute trades efficiently and quickly. They can process large volumes of data and execute orders at high speeds, which helps reduce trading costs and market impact.

2. **Liquidity Provision:** Many algorithms, such as market makers, provide liquidity to markets by continuously quoting bid and ask prices. They are designed to profit from the spread between these prices while ensuring that there are always tradable prices available for buyers and sellers.

3. **Execution Quality:** Execution algorithms aim to achieve the best possible execution price for a given trade. They take into account factors like market conditions, order size, and urgency to optimize execution outcomes.

4. **Arbitrage:** Arbitrage algorithms seek to profit from price discrepancies between different markets or instruments. They can identify and exploit price differentials that may exist for only brief moments.

5. **Statistical Analysis:** Some algorithms employ statistical models to identify patterns or anomalies in market data. These algorithms can be used for strategies such as statistical arbitrage or trend following.

6. **Risk Management:** Algorithms play a crucial role in risk management. They can monitor positions in real-time, implement stop-loss orders, and dynamically adjust trading strategies to limit potential losses.

7. **Market Access:** Algorithms provide market access to a wide range of participants, from individual retail traders to large institutional investors. This democratization of market access has expanded opportunities for traders.

8. **Automated Trading:** Algorithms enable automated trading, which eliminates emotional biases and ensures consistent execution of trading strategies. Traders can define precise entry and exit criteria, allowing for disciplined trading.

9. **High-Frequency Trading (HFT):** High-frequency trading algorithms execute a large number of trades in extremely short timeframes. They capitalize on small price differentials and market inefficiencies, contributing to market liquidity and efficiency.

10. **Machine Learning and AI:** Modern algorithms increasingly incorporate machine learning and AI techniques to make more adaptive and data-driven trading decisions. These algorithms can analyze vast amounts of data to identify complex patterns and trading opportunities.

11. **Regulatory Compliance:** Algorithms must comply with regulatory rules and requirements. Compliance algorithms help monitor trading activity to ensure it aligns with regulatory standards, preventing market abuse and ensuring fair trading practices.

12. **Market Surveillance:** Market surveillance algorithms are used by exchanges and regulators to monitor trading activity for unusual or potentially manipulative behavior. They help maintain market integrity and detect irregularities.

13. **Market Stability:** Algorithms can contribute to market stability by quickly adapting to changing market conditions and absorbing trading volume, helping prevent extreme price fluctuations.

14. **Market Fragmentation:** The proliferation of algorithms has contributed to market fragmentation, with trading occurring on multiple venues and dark pools. This has raised questions about market structure and transparency.

15. **Risk of Technology Glitches:** While algorithms offer many benefits, they also introduce the risk of technology glitches, such as flash crashes or erroneous trades. Regulatory safeguards are in place to mitigate these risks.

Algorithms have become indispensable tools in modern financial markets. They enhance market efficiency, liquidity, and accessibility while presenting challenges related to market structure, regulation, and technology risks. As technology continues to advance, the role of algorithms in financial markets is likely to evolve further, shaping the future of trading and investment.

Algorithmic trading offers various benefits and advantages to market participants, but it also comes with its own set of challenges and risks. Here's an overview of the benefits and challenges of algorithmic trading:

Benefits of Algorithmic Trading:

1. **Efficiency:** Algorithms can execute trades with precision and speed, reducing the time and cost associated with manual trading. This efficiency is particularly valuable in markets with high trading volumes.

2. **Lower Transaction Costs:** Algorithmic trading can minimize transaction costs by optimizing order execution and achieving better prices. Algorithms can execute orders in a way that minimizes market impact and slippage.

3. **Increased Liquidity:** Market-making algorithms contribute to market liquidity by continuously quoting bid and ask prices. This makes it easier for buyers and sellers to find counterparties and execute trades.

4. **Diversification:** Algorithms allow traders to diversify their strategies across various asset classes, markets, and timeframes, reducing exposure to specific risks.

5. **Risk Management:** Algorithmic trading systems can incorporate risk management measures, such as stop-loss orders and position limits, to protect capital and minimize losses.

6. **Consistency:** Algorithms execute trades based on predefined rules, eliminating emotional biases and ensuring consistent trading decisions.

7. **Backtesting:** Traders can backtest algorithms using historical data to assess their performance and refine strategies before deploying them in live markets.

8. **Accessibility:** Algorithmic trading is accessible to a wide range of market participants, from individual retail traders to large institutional investors.

9. **Market Access:** Algorithms provide access to multiple markets and trading venues, enabling traders to capitalize on opportunities worldwide.

10. **Real-time Monitoring:** Traders can monitor their algorithmic strategies in real-time and make adjustments as needed to adapt to changing market conditions.

Challenges and Risks of Algorithmic Trading:

1. **Technology Risks:** Algorithmic trading relies on complex technology systems that are susceptible to glitches, latency issues, and software failures. These can lead to substantial losses or market disruptions.

2. **Regulatory Compliance:** Compliance with regulatory requirements can be challenging, as algorithms need to adhere to rules related to market manipulation, circuit breakers, and reporting.

3. **Over-Optimization:** Over-optimizing algorithms based on historical data can lead to strategies that perform well in the past but poorly in the future (overfitting).

4. **Market Impact:** Aggressive algorithmic strategies can lead to significant market impact, causing prices to move against the trader's position and eroding potential profits.

5. **Contagion Risk:** In times of market stress or unexpected events, algorithms can amplify market movements and contribute to increased volatility.

6. **Lack of Transparency:** Some algorithmic trading strategies are highly proprietary and lack transparency, which can make it difficult for regulators and market participants to understand their impact on markets.

7. **Competition:** As algorithmic trading becomes more widespread, competition among algorithmic traders intensifies, potentially reducing profit margins.

8. **Market Fragmentation:** Algorithmic trading has contributed to market fragmentation, with trading occurring across various venues and dark pools. This can complicate trade execution and reporting.

9. **Human Oversight:** While algorithms are automated, human oversight is essential to monitor their performance, make strategic adjustments, and intervene in exceptional circumstances.

10. **Ethical Concerns:** Some algorithmic trading practices, especially in high-frequency trading, raise ethical concerns about fairness and market manipulation.

Algorithmic trading offers numerous advantages in terms of efficiency, cost reduction, and risk management. However, it also introduces technology and regulatory challenges, market impact risks, and concerns about market integrity and transparency. Traders and institutions engaging in algorithmic trading must carefully balance the benefits with the associated risks and adopt robust risk management practices to navigate the complexities of modern financial markets.

Chapter 2: Algorithmic Trading Strategies

Common Algorithmic Trading Strategies

Algorithmic trading strategies come in a wide variety, each designed to exploit specific market conditions and opportunities. Here are some common algorithmic trading strategies used in modern financial markets:

1. **Market Making:** Market makers use algorithms to continuously quote bid and ask prices for a particular asset. They profit from the spread—the difference between the buying and selling prices. Market-making algorithms help maintain liquidity by providing traders with readily available prices.

2. **Arbitrage Strategies:** a. **Statistical Arbitrage:** This strategy identifies mispricing between related assets based on statistical models. When the price relationship deviates from historical norms, the algorithm executes trades to capitalize on the expected convergence. b. **Pairs Trading:** Pairs trading involves trading two correlated assets simultaneously. When the price relationship between the two assets diverges, the algorithm buys the underperforming asset and sells the outperforming one, aiming to profit from the reversion to the mean.

3. **Trend Following:** Trend-following algorithms aim to capitalize on established market trends. They analyze price and volume data to identify upward or downward trends and enter positions in the direction of the trend.

4. **Mean Reversion:** Mean reversion strategies assume that prices will eventually return to their historical averages or mean levels. Algorithms

identify assets that have deviated significantly from their mean and execute trades to profit from the expected reversion.

5. **Algorithmic Scalping:** Scalping algorithms aim to profit from small, short-term price fluctuations. They execute a large number of trades with minimal holding periods, often capturing tiny profit margins on each trade.

6. **Volume Weighted Average Price (VWAP):** VWAP algorithms aim to execute trades at an average price that closely matches the asset's average trading volume for a specified period. This minimizes market impact when executing large orders.

7. **Time-Weighted Average Price (TWAP):** Similar to VWAP, TWAP algorithms aim to spread trade execution evenly over a specified time period, minimizing market impact. TWAP strategies are often used for less liquid assets.

8. **Sniper or Iceberg Orders:** Sniper algorithms execute orders stealthily by placing small, visible orders in the market while hiding a larger order in the order book. This strategy reduces market impact and avoids signaling intentions.

9. **Machine Learning and AI-Based Strategies:** Algorithms that incorporate machine learning and artificial intelligence analyze large datasets to identify patterns, anomalies, and trading opportunities. These strategies can be highly adaptive and data-driven.

10. **Sentiment Analysis:** Sentiment analysis algorithms process news, social media, and other sources of market sentiment to make trading decisions. They seek to gauge market sentiment and trade accordingly.

11. **Options Market-Making:** Options market-makers use algorithms to quote bid and ask prices for options contracts. They adjust their

quotes based on factors like volatility and underlying asset price movements.

12. **Execution Algorithms:** These algorithms focus on optimizing the execution of large orders. They aim to minimize market impact and slippage by intelligently slicing and timing order execution.

13. **Algo Wheels:** Algo wheels are algorithms that dynamically select and execute trades with various brokers or venues based on factors like pricing, execution speed, and order size.

14. **Smart Order Routing (SOR):** SOR algorithms route orders to different trading venues to achieve the best execution price. They consider factors such as order size, market conditions, and fees.

15. **Market On Close (MOC) and Limit On Close (LOC) Orders:** These algorithms are designed to execute trades at the closing price of the trading session, contributing to the benchmark price and allowing investors to adjust their portfolios.

16. **High-Frequency Trading (HFT) Strategies:** High-frequency trading algorithms execute a large number of orders in extremely short timeframes, capitalizing on market inefficiencies and exploiting price differentials that exist for fractions of a second.

17. **Multi-Asset Strategies:** Some algorithms trade across multiple asset classes, including equities, fixed income, currencies, and commodities, in search of diversified trading opportunities.

These are just a few examples of the many algorithmic trading strategies available. Traders and institutions choose strategies based on their objectives, risk tolerance, and the market conditions they seek to exploit. Successful algorithmic trading often involves a combination of strategies, risk management techniques, and ongoing adaptation to changing market dynamics.

Trend-following and mean-reversion are two contrasting algorithmic trading strategies that exploit different market dynamics. Here's a comparison of these two strategies:

Trend-Following Strategies:

1. **Objective:** Trend-following strategies aim to identify and capitalize on existing market trends. These trends can be upward (bullish) or downward (bearish).

2. **Assumption:** Trend-following assumes that markets have momentum, meaning that assets that have been rising will continue to rise, and those that have been falling will continue to fall for a certain period.

3. **Trading Logic:** Trend-following algorithms typically use technical indicators, moving averages, and momentum indicators to identify and confirm trends. When a trend is identified, the algorithm enters positions in the direction of the trend.

4. **Risk Management:** Risk management in trend-following strategies often involves setting stop-loss orders to limit potential losses if the trend reverses. Traders may also use trailing stops to lock in profits as the trend progresses.

5. **Timeframe:** Trend-following strategies can vary in timeframe, from short-term intraday trends to long-term trends spanning weeks or months.

6. **Market Conditions:** Trend-following strategies tend to perform well in strongly trending markets but can suffer losses in choppy or range-bound markets with no clear trend.

7. **Example:** A trend-following algorithm might buy a stock when its 50-day moving average crosses above its 200-day moving average, indicating a bullish trend.

Mean-Reversion Strategies:

1. **Objective:** Mean-reversion strategies aim to profit from the belief that asset prices will revert to their historical mean or average price after deviating from it.

2. **Assumption:** Mean-reversion assumes that markets exhibit short-term price fluctuations around a stable long-term equilibrium, and extreme deviations from this equilibrium are likely to reverse.

3. **Trading Logic:** Mean-reversion algorithms often use statistical techniques to identify overbought or oversold conditions. When an asset's price deviates significantly from its historical mean, the algorithm enters positions betting on a reversion to the mean.

4. **Risk Management:** Risk management in mean-reversion strategies may involve setting stop-loss orders to limit losses in case the asset's price continues to move away from the mean.

5. **Timeframe:** Mean-reversion strategies can operate on various timeframes, from intraday to longer-term horizons.

6. **Market Conditions:** Mean-reversion strategies perform well in range-bound or sideways markets where prices frequently oscillate around a central value. They may struggle in strongly trending markets.

7. **Example:** A mean-reversion algorithm might sell a stock when its Relative Strength Index (RSI) crosses above 70, indicating overbought conditions, and buy when it crosses below 30, indicating oversold conditions.

Key Differences:

1. **Market View:** Trend-following strategies are based on the belief that trends persist, while mean-reversion strategies assume that prices revert to the mean.

2. **Indicators:** Trend-following strategies use momentum and trend indicators, while mean-reversion strategies use oscillators and statistical measures.

3. **Performance:** Trend-following strategies tend to perform well in strong trends but poorly in sideways markets, while mean-reversion strategies are the opposite.

4. **Risk Management:** Risk management in trend-following strategies focuses on limiting losses if trends reverse, whereas in mean-reversion strategies, it aims to manage the risk of continued extreme price movements.

5. **Psychology:** Trend-following aligns with the idea of "the trend is your friend," while mean-reversion can be seen as contrarian, betting against prevailing market sentiment.

Both strategies have their merits, and their suitability depends on market conditions, the trader's risk tolerance, and the specific assets being traded. Some traders even use a combination of both strategies to diversify their trading approach.

High-frequency and low-frequency trading strategies are two distinct approaches to algorithmic trading, differing primarily in terms of trading speed, frequency, and the types of opportunities they aim to exploit. Here's a comparison of these two strategies:

High-Frequency Trading (HFT) Strategies:

1. **Speed and Frequency:** HFT strategies are characterized by their extremely high speed and frequency of trading. HFT firms execute

a large number of trades in fractions of a second, often within microseconds or milliseconds.

2. **Market Access:** HFT firms typically co-locate their servers in proximity to exchanges to reduce latency (network delay) and gain a speed advantage. They also invest heavily in high-speed data feeds and technology infrastructure.

3. **Trading Opportunities:** HFT strategies focus on exploiting small price differentials, market inefficiencies, and arbitrage opportunities that exist for very short periods. They thrive on market microstructure intricacies.

4. **Market Liquidity:** HFT firms contribute to market liquidity by frequently providing bid and ask quotes. They are often involved in market-making, ensuring that there are always tradable prices available.

5. **Risk Management:** HFT strategies incorporate sophisticated risk management systems to monitor and control trading activities in real-time. They often have automated mechanisms to limit losses and reduce exposure.

6. **Market Impact:** While HFT strategies are designed to minimize market impact, the sheer volume of orders they execute can sometimes contribute to short-lived price fluctuations and increased market volatility.

7. **Assets Traded:** HFT is most common in highly liquid markets like equities, futures, and currency pairs. It is less prevalent in illiquid or less electronically traded markets.

Low-Frequency Strategies:

1. **Speed and Frequency:** Low-frequency strategies, as the name suggests, involve a lower rate of trading activity. Trades can occur over

longer timeframes, ranging from minutes to days, weeks, or even months.

2. **Market Access:** Low-frequency traders do not require the same level of high-speed infrastructure as HFT firms. They can execute trades using standard brokerage platforms.

3. **Trading Opportunities:** Low-frequency strategies are often based on fundamental analysis, technical analysis, or quantitative models. They aim to capitalize on longer-term market trends, macroeconomic factors, or valuation discrepancies.

4. **Market Liquidity:** Low-frequency traders do not contribute significantly to intraday market liquidity. Their trades are typically larger in size and aimed at taking advantage of longer-term trends.

5. **Risk Management:** Risk management is crucial in low-frequency trading, as positions are held for more extended periods. Traders employ stop-loss orders, portfolio diversification, and position-sizing rules to manage risk.

6. **Market Impact:** Low-frequency trading typically has a more noticeable market impact than HFT, especially when executing large orders. Traders may need to be patient and execute trades carefully to avoid impacting prices.

7. **Assets Traded:** Low-frequency strategies can be applied to a wide range of assets, including stocks, bonds, commodities, options, and more. They are often used in less liquid markets where long-term trends are more pronounced.

Key Differences:

1. **Speed:** The most significant difference is the speed of trading. HFT operates at ultra-high speeds, while low-frequency trading is much slower.

2. **Trading Opportunities:** HFT strategies focus on exploiting short-lived price discrepancies, while low-frequency strategies aim to capture longer-term trends or valuation disparities.

3. **Market Impact:** HFT strategies aim to minimize market impact, whereas low-frequency trading can have a more noticeable impact on prices, especially with large orders.

4. **Infrastructure:** HFT requires specialized infrastructure and co-location services, while low-frequency trading can be conducted using standard brokerage platforms.

5. **Risk:** Low-frequency trading tends to involve more extended exposure to market risk, while HFT focuses on minimizing risk through rapid execution and short holding periods.

Traders and institutions choose between high-frequency and low-frequency strategies based on their risk tolerance, capital, technology capabilities, and the specific market conditions they seek to exploit. Some firms also employ a hybrid approach, using a mix of strategies to diversify their trading activities.

Statistical arbitrage and pairs trading are both quantitative trading strategies that aim to profit from statistical relationships between two or more assets. While they share similarities, they have distinct characteristics and approaches. Here's an explanation of each strategy:

Statistical Arbitrage:

1. **Objective:** Statistical arbitrage, often abbreviated as stat arb, is a quantitative trading strategy that seeks to exploit short-term pricing inefficiencies or mispricings between related assets or securities.

2. **Assumption:** Stat arb assumes that, over time, the prices of related assets tend to revert to a stable relationship or spread. When this relationship deviates significantly from historical norms, it presents an opportunity to trade.

3. **Trading Logic:** Stat arb algorithms use statistical models and mathematical techniques to identify assets that are temporarily mispriced. These models can be based on cointegration, correlation, or other statistical measures.

4. **Pairs Selection:** Stat arb typically involves pairs of assets, but it can extend to multiple assets. Pairs are selected based on historical price relationships and statistical tests to determine their co-movement.

5. **Trade Execution:** When a stat arb algorithm identifies a spread that has deviated significantly from its historical average or a predefined threshold, it will initiate a trade. This trade could involve buying the undervalued asset and selling the overvalued one.

6. **Risk Management:** Stat arb strategies usually employ risk management measures like stop-loss orders, position sizing, and risk limits to control potential losses.

7. **Time Horizon:** Stat arb strategies typically have a short- to medium-term time horizon and may involve holding positions for hours, days, or weeks.

Pairs Trading:

1. **Objective:** Pairs trading is a specific form of statistical arbitrage that seeks to profit from the relative price movements between two

correlated assets. It assumes that the spread between the assets will revert to a mean value over time.

2. **Assumption:** Pairs trading assumes that the selected pair of assets has a stable long-term relationship, and any deviations from this relationship are temporary and will eventually converge.

3. **Trading Logic:** Pairs trading algorithms continuously monitor the prices of the two assets in the pair. When the spread between them deviates significantly from its historical mean, the algorithm will take action.

4. **Pairs Selection:** Pairs trading involves selecting two assets that have a high degree of historical correlation. Popular pairs might include two stocks from the same industry or two related commodities.

5. **Trade Execution:** When the spread widens beyond a certain threshold, the pairs trading algorithm will enter a long position in the undervalued asset and a short position in the overvalued asset. It holds these positions until the spread narrows.

6. **Risk Management:** Pairs trading strategies employ risk management measures like stop-loss orders, position sizing, and hedging to manage risk.

7. **Time Horizon:** Pairs trading typically has a short- to medium-term time horizon, with positions held until the spread reverts to its historical mean.

Key Differences:

1. **Scope:** Statistical arbitrage encompasses a broader range of strategies, while pairs trading is a specific subset focused on trading pairs of correlated assets.

2. **Asset Selection:** Stat arb can involve multiple assets, whereas pairs trading always involves trading a pair of assets.

3. **Trading Logic:** Stat arb can use various statistical relationships, not limited to correlations, whereas pairs trading specifically relies on the correlation between two assets.

4. **Trade Execution:** Stat arb may involve buying and selling multiple assets simultaneously, while pairs trading always involves buying one asset and selling the other in the pair.

5. **Flexibility:** Stat arb is more flexible in terms of asset selection, whereas pairs trading is limited to the selection of correlated pairs.

Statistical arbitrage is a broader strategy that encompasses various quantitative approaches, while pairs trading is a subset of stat arb that focuses exclusively on trading pairs of correlated assets based on their relative price movements. Both strategies require rigorous statistical analysis and risk management to be successful.

Chapter 3: Data and Technology in Algorithmic Trading

Data Sources and Types for Trading Algorithms

Data is the lifeblood of algorithmic trading, and the quality and variety of data sources play a crucial role in the success of trading algorithms. Trading algorithms rely on a wide range of data types to make informed decisions. Here are some common data sources and types used in algorithmic trading:

1. **Market Data:**

◈ **Real-Time Price Data:** This includes bid and ask prices, trade prices, and trading volumes for various financial instruments, such as stocks, currencies, commodities, and derivatives.

◈ **Order Book Data:** Detailed information about the current state of the order book, including the depth of bids and offers at various price levels.

◈ **Tick Data:** Time-stamped data that records every price change, trade, or order book update at the highest granularity, often in milliseconds or microseconds.

◈ **Historical Price Data:** Archived data that provides historical price and trading volume information, essential for backtesting and strategy development.

2. **Fundamental Data:**

◈ **Financial Statements:** Company financials, including income statements, balance sheets, and cash flow statements, used for fundamental analysis of stocks.

◈ **Economic Indicators:** Data on economic factors such as GDP growth, inflation rates, employment figures, and consumer sentiment, which impact currency, equity, and commodity markets.

◈ **Corporate Actions:** Information on events like dividends, stock splits, mergers, and acquisitions that can affect the price and fundamentals of a security.

3. **News and Sentiment Data:**

◈ **News Feeds:** Real-time news sources providing financial news, earnings reports, geopolitical developments, and other events that can influence market sentiment.

◈ **Social Media Sentiment:** Data from social media platforms and online forums, often analyzed using natural language processing (NLP) techniques to gauge market sentiment.

4. **Alternative Data:**

◈ **Alternative data sources:** These include non-traditional data sources such as satellite imagery, credit card transaction data, foot traffic data, and more. Alternative data can provide unique insights into various industries and markets.

5. **Volatility and Implied Volatility Data:**

◈ **Volatility Measures:** Data related to historical volatility, implied volatility, and options pricing, which are crucial for options trading and volatility-based strategies.

6. **Exchange Data and Market Feeds:**

◈ **Direct Market Feeds:** Data feeds provided directly by stock exchanges, futures exchanges, and other trading venues, offering the most up-to-date information.

◈ **Consolidated Feeds:** Aggregated data feeds that combine information from multiple exchanges, offering a broader view of market activity.

7. **Macro and Micro Economic Data:**

◈ **Government Reports:** Data releases by government agencies, such as employment reports, interest rate decisions, and trade balance figures, which can impact financial markets.

8. **Technical Indicators:**

◈ **Moving Averages:** Data used to calculate various moving averages, which are commonly used technical indicators in algorithmic trading.

◈ **Relative Strength Index (RSI):** Historical price and volume data used to calculate oscillators like RSI, Stochastic Oscillator, and MACD (Moving Average Convergence Divergence).

9. **Option Data:**

◈ **Options Chains:** Information on available options contracts, including strike prices, expiration dates, implied volatilities, and open interest.

10. **Execution Data:**

◈ **Order Execution Data:** Records of order execution details, including timestamps, fill prices, and order type.

11. **Risk Data:**

◈ **Position Data:** Information on current positions, including size, open price, and unrealized profit/loss.

◈ **Market Risk Data:** Data related to market risk factors, including beta, value at risk (VaR), and stress testing parameters.

12. **Machine Learning Data:**

◈ **Training Data:** Historical data used for training machine learning models, including features and target variables.

◈ **Test Data:** Data used to evaluate the performance of machine learning models.

13. **Geographic and Weather Data:**

◈ **Geographic Information Systems (GIS):** Geographic data that can be used for location-based trading strategies, such as weather-based trading.

14. **Market Microstructure Data:**

◈ **Order Flow Data:** Information on the flow of orders, including order submission, cancellation, and execution data.

15. **Blockchain and Cryptocurrency Data:**

◈ **Blockchain Data:** Data from blockchain networks, including transaction history, block data, and cryptocurrency prices.

Effective data management, including data cleaning, normalization, and storage, is essential for utilizing these data sources effectively in algorithmic trading strategies. Additionally, trading firms often invest in high-speed data feeds, data analytics platforms, and data warehouses to support their algorithmic trading operations.

Data processing and cleaning are essential steps in preparing data for use in algorithmic trading strategies. Clean, accurate, and well-structured data is crucial for making informed trading decisions and avoiding errors. Here are the key steps and considerations for data processing and cleaning in algorithmic trading:

1. Data Collection:

◈ Gather data from various sources, including market data feeds, fundamental data providers, news sources, and any other relevant sources specific to your trading strategy.

2. Data Integration:

◈ Combine data from multiple sources into a unified dataset, ensuring that data is properly aligned and timestamps are synchronized. Data integration may involve data normalization to a common time zone.

3. Data Validation:

◈ Check data for completeness and consistency. Look for missing values, duplicate records, and outliers that may skew analysis and trading decisions.

4. Data Cleaning:

◈ Identify and address data errors, such as incorrect or inconsistent values. Common data cleaning tasks include:

◈ Removing duplicate records.

◈ Filling missing values through interpolation or estimation.

◈ Correcting erroneous data entries.

◈ Handling outliers by either removing them or transforming them to mitigate their impact.

5. Time Series Alignment:

◈ Ensure that time series data (e.g., price and volume data) is correctly aligned across different datasets. This alignment is critical for accurate analysis and modeling.

6. Handling Corporate Actions:

◈ Adjust historical price and volume data to account for corporate actions such as stock splits, dividends, and mergers, which can impact historical data accuracy.

7. Data Quality Checks:

◈ Implement data quality checks to monitor the integrity of incoming data in real-time. This includes checking for data gaps, inconsistencies, or unusual patterns.

8. Data Aggregation and Resampling:

◈ Depending on the strategy and data frequency, aggregate or resample data into the desired timeframes (e.g., minute, hourly, daily) to match the strategy's trading frequency.

9. Data Storage and Management:

◈ Organize and store data in a structured and efficient manner, such as in databases or data warehouses, for easy retrieval and analysis.

10. Backtesting Considerations: - Ensure that cleaned and processed historical data is suitable for backtesting algorithms. This may involve accounting for slippage, transaction costs, and realistic execution delays.

11. Data Feeds and Real-Time Processing: - Implement robust data feed mechanisms for real-time data processing, including handling data updates, handling disconnections, and error recovery.

12. Data Versioning and Auditing: - Implement data versioning and auditing practices to keep track of changes in data sources and processing pipelines, helping to maintain data quality and traceability.

13. Monitoring and Alerting: - Continuously monitor data quality in real-time and set up alerts for anomalies or issues in the data. This proactive approach can help identify and address problems quickly.

14. Documentation: - Maintain detailed documentation of data sources, processing steps, and cleaning procedures. Documentation is essential for transparency, reproducibility, and compliance.

15. Quality Assurance Testing: - Periodically validate the accuracy and quality of the cleaned and processed data through quality assurance testing and data reconciliation.

Effective data processing and cleaning are ongoing tasks in algorithmic trading, as data quality is critical to the performance and reliability of trading strategies. Robust data management practices and automated data validation procedures are essential for maintaining the integrity of trading data throughout its lifecycle.

Hardware and infrastructure considerations are crucial for the success of algorithmic trading operations. The choice of hardware and the design of the trading infrastructure can significantly impact trading speed, reliability, and overall performance. Here are key considerations for hardware and infrastructure in algorithmic trading:

1. Low Latency: Achieving low-latency trading is a top priority for many algorithmic traders. Low latency refers to minimizing the time delay between receiving market data and executing orders. Critical components for achieving low latency include:

◈ **High-Frequency Network:** Use high-speed, dedicated data lines and network infrastructure to reduce data transmission times.

◈ **Low-Latency Hardware:** Employ specialized servers and hardware components optimized for low-latency trading, including CPUs, memory, and network cards.

◈ **Co-Location:** Co-locate trading servers near exchange servers to reduce network latency and gain a speed advantage.

2. Redundancy and Failover: Trading systems must be highly reliable. Redundant hardware and failover mechanisms ensure uninterrupted trading operations in case of hardware failures or network disruptions.

3. Scalability: Trading infrastructure should be scalable to accommodate growing trading volumes and the addition of new strategies or assets. Scalability includes both hardware and software components.

4. Data Storage: Effective data storage solutions are essential for storing and accessing historical market data, trade records, and other relevant information. Consider the following:

◈ **Databases:** Use high-performance, scalable databases for data storage and retrieval.

◈ **Data Warehouses:** Store and manage large datasets efficiently using data warehousing solutions.

◈ **Cloud Storage:** Explore cloud-based storage solutions for scalability and redundancy.

5. Risk Management: Implement robust risk management systems and hardware components to monitor trading activities, set position limits, and trigger risk control mechanisms in real-time.

6. Monitoring and Alerting: Set up hardware and software components for real-time monitoring of trading infrastructure. Implement alerts and notifications for issues such as system failures, data feed disruptions, or trading anomalies.

7. **Hardware Redundancy:** Use redundant hardware components, including servers, storage devices, and networking equipment, to ensure high availability and minimize downtime.

8. **High-Performance Computing (HPC):** Consider employing high-performance computing clusters for intensive quantitative analysis and data modeling tasks. HPC can speed up strategy development and backtesting.

9. **Geographic Diversity:** Diversify infrastructure across multiple geographic locations to reduce the risk of regional outages or disruptions.

10. **Data Feeds and Market Access:** Invest in reliable data feeds from exchanges and trading venues. Ensure efficient connectivity for market access, including direct market access (DMA) for executing orders.

11. **Disaster Recovery:** Develop and test a comprehensive disaster recovery plan that includes data backup and recovery procedures, as well as hardware redundancy across multiple locations.

12. **Compliance and Security:** Implement stringent security measures to protect sensitive trading data and ensure compliance with regulatory requirements.

13. **Virtualization and Containerization:** Explore virtualization and containerization technologies to optimize resource utilization and enhance flexibility in deploying trading applications.

14. **High-Performance Storage:** Deploy high-speed, low-latency storage solutions such as solid-state drives (SSDs) for trading systems that require fast data access.

15. Regulatory Compliance: Ensure that hardware and infrastructure configurations meet regulatory compliance requirements, including data retention, reporting, and auditability.

16. Cost Considerations: Balancing the need for high-performance hardware with cost considerations is crucial. Evaluate the cost-effectiveness of hardware choices relative to the trading strategies being employed.

Successful algorithmic trading firms carefully assess their hardware and infrastructure needs to meet their trading objectives while maintaining reliability and scalability. Regular performance testing and infrastructure upgrades are common practices to stay competitive in the fast-paced world of algorithmic trading.

Algorithm development platforms and tools are essential for building, testing, and deploying algorithmic trading strategies. These tools provide the necessary infrastructure, libraries, and frameworks for traders and developers to create, backtest, and execute trading algorithms effectively. Here are some commonly used algorithm development platforms and tools:

1. Python:

◈ **Python:** Python is a popular programming language for algorithmic trading due to its readability, extensive libraries, and community support. Libraries like NumPy, pandas, and scikit-learn are commonly used for data analysis and strategy development.

◈ **Jupyter Notebook:** Jupyter notebooks provide an interactive environment for prototyping and experimenting with trading strategies.

2. R:

◈ **R:** R is another language frequently used for statistical analysis and strategy development in algorithmic trading. It offers a wide range of packages for data analysis and visualization.

3. MATLAB:

◈ **MATLAB:** MATLAB is a high-level programming language and environment commonly used for quantitative analysis, modeling, and strategy development.

4. Algorithmic Trading Libraries:

◈ **QuantConnect:** QuantConnect is an open-source algorithmic trading platform that supports multiple asset classes. It provides access to historical and real-time data, backtesting, and live trading capabilities.

◈ **Backtrader:** Backtrader is a Python-based framework for developing and testing trading strategies. It supports custom indicators, data feeds, and broker integration.

◈ **Zipline:** Zipline is an open-source algorithmic trading library developed by Quantopian. It is designed for event-driven algorithmic trading systems and integrates with QuantConnect.

5. Trading Platforms:

◈ **MetaTrader:** MetaTrader 4 and MetaTrader 5 are popular trading platforms that offer a built-in scripting language, MetaQuotes Language (MQL), for developing custom indicators and automated trading strategies.

◈ **Interactive Brokers (IB) API:** Interactive Brokers provides a powerful API for building and executing algorithmic trading strategies.

It supports various programming languages, including Python, Java, and C++.

6. Machine Learning Frameworks:

◈ **TensorFlow:** TensorFlow is a popular open-source machine learning framework that can be used for developing machine learning-based trading strategies.

◈ **PyTorch:** PyTorch is another machine learning framework with a growing user base in algorithmic trading applications.

7. Data Analysis and Visualization:

◈ **Tableau:** Tableau is a data visualization tool that can be used to create interactive dashboards and visualize trading performance.

◈ **Power BI:** Microsoft Power BI is another tool for data visualization and business intelligence.

8. Cloud Services:

◈ **Amazon Web Services (AWS):** AWS offers a range of cloud computing resources, including virtual machines and data storage, which can be used for backtesting and deploying trading algorithms.

◈ **Google Cloud Platform (GCP):** GCP provides cloud-based infrastructure and machine learning services for algorithmic trading applications.

9. Data Providers:

◈ **Quandl:** Quandl is a data provider that offers a wide range of financial and economic datasets, which can be used for strategy development and analysis.

10. Algorithmic Trading Frameworks: - Algorithmic Trading Frameworks: Some specialized algorithmic trading frameworks like AlgoTrader and OpenAlgo provide end-to-end solutions for building and executing trading strategies.

11. Integrated Development Environments (IDEs): - PyCharm, Visual Studio Code, RStudio: These IDEs offer features such as code debugging, version control, and extensions that facilitate algorithm development.

The choice of platform and tools depends on various factors, including the trader's programming proficiency, preferred programming language, asset class, and strategy complexity. It's common for traders and developers to leverage a combination of these platforms and tools to create, test, and deploy algorithmic trading strategies effectively.

Chapter 4: Building Algorithmic Trading Models

Designing a Trading Algorithm

Designing a trading algorithm is a critical step in algorithmic trading. A well-designed algorithm forms the foundation for a successful trading strategy. Here are the key steps and considerations for designing a trading algorithm:

1. Define Your Objective:

⟐ Start by clearly defining your trading objectives. What is the goal of your algorithm? Are you looking for high-frequency trading, market-making, trend-following, or a different strategy?

2. Choose Your Asset Class:

⟐ Determine the asset class you want to trade, whether it's equities, commodities, forex, options, cryptocurrencies, or a combination. Different asset classes have unique characteristics and require specific strategies.

3. Select a Trading Style:

⟐ Choose a trading style that aligns with your objectives and risk tolerance. Common trading styles include day trading, swing trading, scalping, and position trading.

4. Develop a Hypothesis:

⟐ Formulate a clear hypothesis about the market conditions you believe will lead to profitable trades. Consider factors like technical indicators, fundamental analysis, sentiment analysis, or statistical relationships.

5. Identify Entry and Exit Signals:

◈ Define specific entry and exit criteria for your trades. These criteria may be based on technical indicators (e.g., moving averages, RSI), fundamental analysis (e.g., earnings reports), or a combination of factors.

6. Risk Management:

◈ Implement robust risk management rules to protect your capital. Determine position sizing, stop-loss levels, and take-profit levels based on your risk tolerance and the volatility of the assets you're trading.

7. Backtesting:

◈ Backtest your trading algorithm using historical data to evaluate its performance. Backtesting helps you assess how your strategy would have performed in the past and identify potential weaknesses.

8. Optimization:

◈ Fine-tune your algorithm based on the results of backtesting. Optimization may involve adjusting parameters, timeframes, or risk management rules to improve performance.

9. Market Impact Analysis:

◈ Analyze the potential market impact of your algorithm. Consider how your trades may affect market prices, liquidity, and order execution.

10. Data Sources: - Select the data sources and types required for your algorithm. Ensure you have access to high-quality, reliable data, including market data, fundamental data, and news feeds.

11. Technology and Infrastructure: - Choose the appropriate hardware, software, and infrastructure for executing your algorithm. Ensure low latency and high reliability, especially for high-frequency trading.

12. Compliance and Regulation: - Understand and adhere to regulatory requirements and exchange rules that may impact your trading algorithm. Compliance is essential to avoid legal and operational issues.

13. Paper Trading: - Before trading with real capital, conduct paper trading or simulation testing to validate your algorithm's performance in a risk-free environment.

14. Continuous Monitoring and Adaptation: - After deploying your algorithm, continuously monitor its performance in live markets. Be prepared to adapt and refine your algorithm based on changing market conditions.

15. Risk Mitigation: - Develop contingency plans for unexpected events or market shocks. Consider circuit breakers, stop-loss mechanisms, and portfolio diversification to mitigate risk.

16. Documentation: - Maintain detailed documentation of your algorithm, including its design, parameters, and performance. Documentation is crucial for compliance, auditability, and troubleshooting.

17. Real-Time Testing: - Conduct real-time testing with a small portion of your capital before deploying the algorithm with a larger investment. This helps identify any issues that may not have surfaced during backtesting.

18. Scale Gradually: - If your algorithm performs well in live markets, consider scaling up gradually to manage risk and avoid overexposure.

Designing a trading algorithm requires a systematic and disciplined approach. It's essential to thoroughly research, test, and iterate on your algorithm to increase the likelihood of success in the competitive world of algorithmic trading. Additionally, staying informed about market developments and continually improving your trading strategies is key to long-term success.

Backtesting and simulation are critical steps in the development and evaluation of algorithmic trading strategies. These processes allow traders to assess how a trading strategy would have performed using historical data and help identify potential strengths and weaknesses. Here's an overview of backtesting and simulation in algorithmic trading:

Backtesting:

1. **Definition:** Backtesting involves applying a trading strategy to historical market data to evaluate its performance and profitability. It assesses how the strategy would have performed if it had been used in the past.

2. **Data Selection:** Choose relevant historical data, including price, volume, and other relevant market information. The quality and accuracy of the data are essential.

3. **Timeframe:** Define the timeframe for the backtest, such as daily, hourly, or tick-level data. The choice of timeframe depends on the strategy's intended trading frequency.

4. **Implementation:** Code the trading strategy in a backtesting platform or programming environment. The code should include entry and exit signals, risk management rules, and transaction costs.

5. **Simulation:** Execute the strategy on historical data, following the trading rules defined in the code. Track the trades, position sizes, and account balance throughout the backtest.

6. **Performance Metrics:** Calculate key performance metrics, such as returns, risk-adjusted returns (e.g., Sharpe ratio), drawdowns, win-loss ratios, and various risk measures.

7. **Analysis:** Analyze the backtest results to assess the strategy's performance. Consider factors like profitability, consistency, volatility, and risk management effectiveness.

8. **Optimization:** If necessary, fine-tune the strategy based on the backtest results. This may involve adjusting parameters, risk management rules, or trading conditions.

9. **Overfitting Risk:** Be cautious of overfitting, where a strategy is tailored too closely to historical data and may not perform well in real-time. Use out-of-sample data to validate the strategy's robustness.

10. **Out-of-Sample Testing:** Validate the strategy on a separate dataset or time period not used in the initial backtest. This helps confirm that the strategy is not overfitting to historical data.

Simulation:

1. **Definition:** Simulation involves running a trading strategy in a controlled environment, often referred to as a "paper trading" or "demo" environment, to assess its real-time performance without risking capital.

2. **Real-Time Conditions:** Simulated trading environments mimic real-time market conditions, including market data feeds, order execution, and transaction costs.

3. **Testing:** Execute the trading strategy in the simulation environment as if it were being traded with real capital. Track trades, order fills, and portfolio performance.

4. **Realistic Testing:** Simulations aim to replicate the trading experience as closely as possible, allowing traders to assess the strategy's execution quality and performance under real-world conditions.

5. **Learning and Refinement:** Simulated trading provides an opportunity to learn how the strategy behaves in practice and make necessary adjustments before trading with real capital.

6. **Risk-Free Testing:** Since no real money is at risk in simulations, they are a safe way to test and refine strategies without incurring losses.

Both backtesting and simulation are essential steps in the algorithmic trading development process. They help traders gain confidence in their strategies, identify potential issues, and refine their approaches before deploying capital in live markets. However, it's crucial to recognize that past performance does not guarantee future success, and ongoing monitoring and adaptation are necessary as market conditions change.

Risk management is a critical aspect of algorithmic trading. It involves the identification, assessment, and mitigation of risks associated with trading algorithms and the capital allocated to them. Effective risk management helps protect capital, minimize losses, and ensure the long-term viability of algorithmic trading strategies. Here are key components of risk management in algorithmic trading:

1. Position Sizing:

◈ Determine the size of each position based on factors such as risk tolerance, capital available, and strategy characteristics. Position sizing should aim to limit the potential loss on any single trade to a predetermined percentage of the trading capital.

2. Stop Loss Orders:

◈ Implement stop loss orders to automatically exit a trade if it reaches a predefined price level. Stop losses help limit losses on individual trades and prevent catastrophic drawdowns.

3. Take Profit Orders:

◈ Use take profit orders to automatically exit a trade when it reaches a predetermined profit target. This helps lock in profits and avoid giving back gains.

4. Risk-Reward Ratio:

◈ Evaluate the risk-reward ratio for each trade. Ensure that the potential reward justifies the risk taken. A commonly used guideline is to aim for a risk-reward ratio of at least 1:2.

5. Portfolio Diversification:

◈ Diversify the trading portfolio by spreading risk across multiple assets or trading strategies. A diversified portfolio can help reduce the impact of poor performance in one asset or strategy.

6. Correlation Analysis:

◈ Assess the correlation between assets in the portfolio. Avoid overconcentration in correlated assets, as this can amplify losses during adverse market conditions.

7. Leverage Control:

◈ Use leverage judiciously. High leverage can amplify both gains and losses, so it's important to manage leverage levels to align with risk tolerance.

8. Risk-Based Position Sizing:

◈ Implement risk-based position sizing, where the size of each position is adjusted based on the perceived risk of the trade or market conditions.

9. Risk Parity:

◈ Apply risk parity principles to balance risk across different components of the portfolio, aiming for an equal contribution of risk from each component.

10. Maximum Drawdown Limits: - Set maximum drawdown limits for the trading strategy. This defines the level of loss that is acceptable before the strategy is halted or reevaluated.

11. Stress Testing: - Conduct stress tests to assess how the trading strategy would perform under extreme market conditions. This helps identify vulnerabilities and potential risks.

12. Risk Monitoring: - Continuously monitor the risk exposure of the trading portfolio in real-time. Implement risk management alerts and triggers to take action when predefined risk limits are breached.

13. Risk Assessment: - Regularly assess and quantify the risks associated with the trading strategy, including market risk, liquidity risk, counterparty risk, and operational risk.

14. Backtesting Risk Management: - Include risk management rules in the backtesting process to evaluate how they would have impacted the strategy's historical performance.

15. Documentation and Compliance: - Maintain detailed documentation of risk management procedures and compliance with regulatory requirements. Ensure that risk management practices align with applicable regulations.

16. Contingency Plans: - Develop contingency plans and emergency procedures to address unexpected events, technical failures, or market disruptions.

17. Review and Adjust: - Periodically review and adjust risk management parameters based on changing market conditions, strategy performance, and evolving risk profiles.

Effective risk management is a dynamic process that evolves with market conditions and the development of trading strategies. Traders should continuously evaluate and refine their risk management practices to adapt to the ever-changing landscape of algorithmic trading.

Regulatory compliance is a crucial aspect of algorithmic trading, as trading activities are subject to various regulations and oversight to ensure market integrity, fairness, and investor protection. Traders and trading firms engaged in algorithmic trading must adhere to these regulations to avoid legal and financial consequences. Here are key considerations for regulatory compliance in algorithmic trading:

1. Regulatory Framework:

� Understand the regulatory framework governing algorithmic trading in the specific markets and jurisdictions where you operate. Regulations can vary significantly by region and asset class.

2. Licensing and Registration:

◈ Determine whether your trading activities require licenses or registrations, such as broker-dealer licenses or registration as a market maker. Compliance with these requirements is essential to operate legally.

3. Market Access and Connectivity:

◈ Comply with rules related to market access and connectivity, including compliance with exchange rules, circuit breakers, and order types. Ensure that you meet the technical and operational requirements set by trading venues.

4. Pre-Trade Risk Controls:

◈ Implement pre-trade risk controls to prevent erroneous orders or excessive risk-taking. These controls may include order quantity limits, price limits, and maximum order sizes.

5. Algorithm Testing and Certification:

◈ In some jurisdictions, algorithms used for trading may require certification or approval from regulatory authorities. Ensure that your algorithms meet the necessary regulatory standards.

6. Trade Reporting and Surveillance:

◈ Adhere to trade reporting requirements, including the reporting of trade executions, transaction data, and any required order book information. Implement surveillance mechanisms to detect and prevent market manipulation and abusive trading practices.

7. Best Execution:

◈ Comply with best execution requirements by striving to achieve the best possible execution outcomes for client orders. This may involve routing orders to different venues to obtain optimal execution.

8. Fair and Transparent Pricing:

◈ Ensure that your pricing practices are fair and transparent. Avoid manipulative pricing strategies or tactics that could distort market prices.

9. Compliance Infrastructure:

◈ Establish a robust compliance infrastructure within your organization. This includes appointing a compliance officer or team responsible for ensuring adherence to regulatory requirements.

10. Record Keeping: - Maintain detailed records of all trading activities, including order and execution data, communications, and trading decisions. Record keeping is essential for auditability and regulatory reporting.

11. Data Privacy and Security: - Protect client and trading data in compliance with data privacy laws and cybersecurity regulations. Implement security measures to safeguard sensitive information.

12. Algorithmic Trading Policies: - Develop and document algorithmic trading policies and procedures that outline how trading algorithms are designed, tested, and monitored. Ensure that employees are trained in compliance with these policies.

13. Periodic Audits and Reviews: - Conduct periodic audits and reviews of your algorithmic trading activities to identify and rectify compliance issues. Engage external consultants or auditors, if necessary.

14. Regulatory Updates: - Stay informed about regulatory updates and changes in market rules that may impact algorithmic trading. Adjust your compliance practices accordingly.

15. Education and Training: - Train employees and trading staff on regulatory requirements and best practices for compliance in algorithmic trading.

Failure to comply with regulatory requirements can result in fines, penalties, legal actions, and damage to reputation. Therefore, staying informed and actively managing regulatory compliance is essential for the long-term success and sustainability of algorithmic trading operations.

Chapter 5: Market Microstructure and Liquidity

Understanding Market Microstructure

Market microstructure refers to the detailed mechanics and structure of financial markets, including the processes and interactions that occur during trading. Understanding market microstructure is crucial for algorithmic traders, as it provides insights into how markets operate and how trading algorithms can be optimized for different market conditions. Here are key concepts in market microstructure:

1. Order Book:

◈ An order book is a real-time record of buy and sell orders for a particular asset on an exchange. It displays the prices at which traders are willing to buy (bids) and sell (asks) an asset, along with the respective quantities.

2. Order Types:

◈ Various order types are used by traders to interact with the market, including market orders, limit orders, stop orders, and more. Each order type has specific characteristics and implications for execution.

3. Bid-Ask Spread:

◈ The bid-ask spread is the difference between the highest price at which buyers are willing to purchase an asset (bid) and the lowest price at which sellers are willing to sell it (ask). It represents the cost of executing a trade.

4. Liquidity:

◈ Liquidity refers to the ease with which an asset can be bought or sold without causing significant price changes. Highly liquid assets have tight bid-ask spreads, while illiquid assets have wider spreads.

5. Market Impact:

◈ Market impact measures how a large trade order affects the market. Executing a large order can influence the asset's price, potentially resulting in unfavorable execution prices.

6. Market Orders vs. Limit Orders:

◈ Market orders are executed immediately at the current market price, while limit orders are executed only when the market reaches a specified price level. Traders must consider the trade-off between immediacy and price control.

7. Dark Pools:

◈ Dark pools are private trading venues where large institutional investors can execute trades anonymously. They are used to minimize market impact and avoid price slippage.

8. High-Frequency Trading (HFT):

◈ High-frequency trading involves using algorithmic strategies to execute a large number of trades in milliseconds or microseconds. HFT firms seek to profit from small price discrepancies and liquidity imbalances.

9. Market Makers:

◈ Market makers are traders or firms that provide liquidity by continuously quoting bid and ask prices in the market. They profit from the bid-ask spread.

10. Electronic Communication Networks (ECNs): - ECNs are electronic trading platforms that connect buyers and sellers directly. They enable faster execution and often offer access to multiple trading venues.

11. Tick Size and Lot Size: - Tick size is the minimum price increment by which an asset's price can move. Lot size defines the minimum quantity of shares or contracts that can be traded. These parameters vary by asset class and exchange.

12. Price Discovery: - Price discovery is the process by which market participants determine the fair market price of an asset through the interaction of buy and sell orders.

13. Market Data Feeds: - Market data feeds provide real-time information about market activity, including order book updates, trade prices, and volumes. Access to high-quality market data is essential for algorithmic trading.

14. Regulation and Market Surveillance: - Financial markets are subject to regulatory oversight to ensure fairness and integrity. Regulatory bodies monitor market activity and investigate irregularities and market abuses.

Understanding market microstructure is vital for algorithmic traders to design trading strategies that can navigate market dynamics effectively. Different trading algorithms may be more suitable for specific market conditions and asset classes, making a comprehensive understanding of market microstructure essential for success in algorithmic trading.

Order types and execution algorithms are essential components of algorithmic trading strategies. They determine how and when trading orders are executed in the market. The choice of order types and execution algorithms can significantly impact the performance and outcomes of trading strategies. Here are some common order types and execution algorithms used in algorithmic trading:

Order Types:

1. **Market Order:** A market order is executed immediately at the current market price. Market orders ensure quick execution but do not guarantee a specific price.

2. **Limit Order:** A limit order specifies a price at which a trader is willing to buy (limit buy order) or sell (limit sell order) an asset. The order is executed when the market reaches the specified price or better. Limit orders provide price control but may not guarantee execution.

3. **Stop Order:** A stop order becomes a market order when the market reaches a specific trigger price, known as the stop price. It is used to limit losses (stop-loss order) or capture profits (take-profit order).

4. **Stop-Limit Order:** Similar to a stop order, a stop-limit order becomes a limit order when the market reaches the stop price. However, it includes an additional price limit, specifying the worst price at which the order can be executed.

5. **Trailing Stop Order:** A trailing stop order follows the market price by a specified distance (trail amount). If the market moves in a favorable direction, the stop price adjusts accordingly. Trailing stops help lock in profits while allowing room for price fluctuations.

6. **Iceberg Order:** An iceberg order conceals the actual order size by only displaying a portion of it to the market. When one portion is executed, another portion is automatically revealed. This strategy minimizes market impact.

7. **Fill-or-Kill (FOK) Order:** A FOK order requires that the entire order be executed immediately or not at all. If the full order cannot be filled, it is canceled.

8. **Immediate-or-Cancel (IOC) Order:** An IOC order is designed to be executed immediately. Any portion of the order that cannot be filled immediately is canceled.

Execution Algorithms:

1. **VWAP (Volume-Weighted Average Price):** VWAP algorithms aim to execute orders over a specified time period while achieving a price close to the average market price weighted by trading volume.

2. **TWAP (Time-Weighted Average Price):** TWAP algorithms execute orders evenly over a specified time duration, regardless of volume fluctuations. They aim to minimize market impact.

3. **IS (Implementation Shortfall):** IS algorithms aim to minimize the difference between the initial target price and the actual execution price. They take into account historical price movements and market impact.

4. **POV (Percentage of Volume):** POV algorithms aim to execute a fixed percentage of the total trading volume in a given time frame. They adapt to changing market conditions by adjusting order size.

5. **Dark Pool Algorithms:** Dark pool algorithms route orders to private trading venues to execute away from public exchanges. They are used to minimize market impact and information leakage.

6. **Pairs Trading Algorithms:** These algorithms are used for statistical arbitrage and involve trading pairs of correlated assets. They execute buy and sell orders on the two assets based on their historical price relationship.

7. **Market-Making Algorithms:** Market-making algorithms continuously provide liquidity by quoting bid and ask prices. They profit from the bid-ask spread and aim to minimize risk exposure.

8. **Smart Order Routing (SOR):** SOR algorithms automatically route orders to various trading venues to obtain the best execution prices. They consider factors like order size, liquidity, and market conditions.

The choice of order types and execution algorithms depends on the trading strategy, market conditions, and specific objectives. Algorithmic traders often use a combination of these order types and algorithms to optimize trade execution, manage risk, and achieve their trading goals. Additionally, continuous monitoring and adaptation of order execution strategies are essential to respond to changing market dynamics.

Liquidity plays a critical role in determining the effectiveness and risk associated with trading strategies, especially in algorithmic trading. Liquidity refers to the ease with which an asset can be bought or sold in the market without causing significant price changes. The level of liquidity in a particular market or asset can impact various aspects of trading strategies:

1. Execution Speed:

◈ In highly liquid markets, orders can be executed quickly and at or near the current market price. This is advantageous for high-frequency trading (HFT) strategies that rely on rapid execution.

2. Price Slippage:

◈ Liquidity can affect price slippage, which is the difference between the expected execution price and the actual execution price. In illiquid markets, price slippage can be substantial, impacting trading profitability.

3. Market Impact:

◈ Large orders in illiquid markets can have a significant impact on prices. This is known as market impact, and it can result in unfavorable execution prices. Algorithms need to account for market impact when trading in less liquid assets.

4. Strategy Selection:

◈ The level of liquidity often determines the types of strategies that are viable. Highly liquid markets are suitable for strategies like market making and statistical arbitrage, while less liquid markets may require longer timeframes and more patience.

5. Risk Management:

◈ Liquidity influences the risk associated with a trading strategy. In illiquid markets, traders may have difficulty exiting positions quickly, increasing the risk of substantial losses. Effective risk management is crucial in such situations.

6. Transaction Costs:

◈ Liquidity affects transaction costs, including bid-ask spreads and brokerage fees. In less liquid markets, spreads tend to be wider, increasing the cost of trading. This can impact the profitability of a strategy.

7. Slower Entry and Exit:

◈ In illiquid markets, it may take longer to accumulate or exit positions, which can be a challenge for strategies that rely on precise timing.

8. Diversification:

◈ Liquidity considerations influence portfolio diversification. In less liquid markets, it may be challenging to diversify across multiple assets, limiting risk management options.

9. Market Conditions:

◈ Liquidity can vary significantly depending on market conditions, time of day, and economic events. Traders need to adapt their strategies to changing liquidity profiles.

10. Impact on Risk-Reward Profile: - Liquidity constraints can affect the risk-reward profile of a trading strategy. Traders may need to accept lower returns or higher risk levels in less liquid markets.

11. Algorithm Design: - Algorithms need to be specifically designed to navigate different liquidity conditions. For example, in illiquid markets, algorithms may split large orders into smaller chunks to minimize market impact.

12. Trade Size Considerations: - Liquidity influences the size of trades that can be executed. In illiquid markets, traders may need to limit the size of their positions to avoid market disruption.

Liquidity has a profound impact on the choice and execution of trading strategies. Traders must carefully assess the liquidity of the assets they intend to trade and tailor their strategies accordingly. Effective risk management, algorithm design, and adaptability are essential for successfully navigating both highly liquid and less liquid markets.

Slippage and market impact analysis are crucial components of assessing and managing the performance of trading strategies, especially in algorithmic trading. They help traders understand how the execution of orders in the market may deviate from the intended execution price and quantify the impact of trading on market prices. Here's an overview of slippage and market impact analysis:

Slippage:

Slippage refers to the difference between the expected execution price of a trade and the actual price at which the trade is executed. It can occur in both buy and sell orders and can be either positive (favorable) or negative (unfavorable). Slippage occurs due to various factors, including market volatility, liquidity, and the speed of order execution. Here are key points related to slippage:

1. **Causes of Slippage:** Slippage can occur for several reasons, such as:

� Market volatility: Rapid price movements can lead to slippage.

� Order size: Large orders may not find sufficient liquidity at the desired price.

� Latency: Delays in order transmission and execution can result in slippage.

� Liquidity: Illiquid assets are more prone to slippage due to fewer market participants.

2. **Positive and Negative Slippage:** Positive slippage occurs when a trade is executed at a better price than expected, benefiting the trader. Negative slippage is when the execution price is worse than expected, potentially resulting in higher trading costs.

3. **Quantifying Slippage:** Traders quantify slippage by comparing the intended execution price (e.g., the limit order price) with the actual execution price. The difference is expressed in terms of ticks or price units.

4. **Slippage Tolerance:** Traders need to define their slippage tolerance or acceptable slippage levels for different strategies and market conditions. This helps in setting realistic expectations and controlling risk.

Market Impact Analysis:

Market impact analysis assesses how the execution of large orders affects market prices and liquidity. It helps traders understand how their trades influence the market and how to minimize the impact to achieve better execution. Here are key points related to market impact analysis:

1. **Market Impact Components:** Market impact can be divided into two main components:

◈ Immediate impact: The immediate price change caused by the execution of a trade.

◈ Delayed impact: Subsequent price changes that occur due to the information conveyed by the trade.

2. **Measuring Market Impact:** Market impact can be measured using various methods, including:

◈ Volume-weighted average price (VWAP) analysis.

◈ Implementation shortfall analysis, which compares the execution price to a benchmark price.

◈ Order book analysis, which examines order book dynamics before and after trade execution.

3. **Minimizing Market Impact:** Traders use strategies to minimize market impact, such as:

◈ Algorithmic trading algorithms designed to execute large orders with minimal price impact.

◈ Scheduling orders over time to avoid sudden price moves.

◈ Using dark pools or alternative trading venues to execute large orders away from public markets.

4. **Risk Management:** Understanding market impact is crucial for risk management. Traders need to balance the urgency of execution with the potential price impact and associated risks.

5. **Slippage vs. Market Impact:** While slippage primarily focuses on individual trade executions, market impact analysis considers the broader influence of trading activity on market prices and liquidity.

Both slippage and market impact analysis are vital for algorithmic traders to evaluate the performance of their strategies, control risk, and optimize trade execution. These analyses help traders make informed decisions regarding order size, timing, and execution strategies to achieve their trading goals while minimizing adverse market effects.

Chapter 6: Execution Algorithms

Overview of Execution Algorithms

Execution algorithms are a critical component of algorithmic trading strategies. They determine how trading orders are executed in the market, aiming to achieve the best possible execution outcomes while minimizing market impact and transaction costs. Execution algorithms are designed to navigate the complexities of modern financial markets and can be highly customized to suit specific trading objectives. Here's an overview of some common execution algorithms used in algorithmic trading:

1. VWAP (Volume-Weighted Average Price):

◈ VWAP algorithms aim to execute orders over a specified time horizon while achieving a price close to the volume-weighted average market price. They are particularly suited for minimizing market impact in large trades.

2. TWAP (Time-Weighted Average Price):

◈ TWAP algorithms execute orders evenly over a predetermined time period, regardless of trading volume fluctuations. They are designed to distribute orders consistently throughout the trading day.

3. IS (Implementation Shortfall):

◈ IS algorithms seek to minimize the difference between the initial target price and the actual execution price. They consider historical price movements and market impact to optimize trade execution.

4. POV (Percentage of Volume):

◈ POV algorithms aim to execute a fixed percentage of the total trading volume within a specified timeframe. They adapt to market conditions by adjusting order size.

5. Dark Pool Algorithms:

◈ Dark pool algorithms route orders to private trading venues (dark pools) to execute away from public exchanges. They are used to minimize market impact and information leakage.

6. Market-Making Algorithms:

◈ Market-making algorithms continuously provide liquidity by quoting bid and ask prices. They profit from the bid-ask spread and aim to minimize risk exposure.

7. Smart Order Routing (SOR):

◈ SOR algorithms automatically route orders to various trading venues to obtain the best execution prices. They consider factors like order size, liquidity, and market conditions.

8. Iceberg Orders:

◈ Iceberg algorithms conceal the actual order size by displaying only a portion of it to the market. When one portion is executed, another is automatically revealed. This strategy minimizes market impact.

9. Pairs Trading Algorithms:

◈ Pairs trading algorithms are used for statistical arbitrage. They execute buy and sell orders on two correlated assets based on their historical price relationship.

10. Sweep Orders: - Sweep algorithms aim to execute orders quickly by sweeping the order book at multiple price levels to capture available liquidity.

11. Sniper Orders: - Sniper algorithms execute orders with precision, often aiming for small price improvements. They are used in highly competitive markets.

12. Arrival Price Algorithms: - Arrival price algorithms aim to execute orders at the price that would have been achieved if the entire order were executed immediately upon arrival in the market.

13. Adaptive Algorithms: - Adaptive algorithms adjust their trading strategies based on real-time market conditions. They are designed to respond dynamically to changing liquidity and volatility.

14. Portfolio Algorithms: - Portfolio algorithms manage the execution of orders across multiple assets or securities in a portfolio, considering correlations and portfolio optimization.

The choice of execution algorithm depends on various factors, including trading objectives, order size, asset class, market conditions, and risk tolerance. Algorithmic traders often use a combination of these algorithms to optimize trade execution, minimize costs, and achieve their desired outcomes in the dynamic and competitive landscape of financial markets. Furthermore, the continuous evolution of execution algorithms reflects ongoing efforts to improve trade execution efficiency and performance.

VWAP (Volume-Weighted Average Price) and TWAP (Time-Weighted Average Price) are two popular execution algorithms used in algorithmic trading. They are designed to help traders execute large orders efficiently while minimizing market impact and achieving benchmark prices. Here's an overview of VWAP and TWAP strategies:

VWAP (Volume-Weighted Average Price):

1. **Objective:** VWAP algorithms aim to execute a trading order over a specified time horizon while achieving an execution price as close to the volume-weighted average market price as possible.

2. **Time Horizon:** VWAP strategies typically span a trading day or a specific time period chosen by the trader. The goal is to distribute the order's execution evenly throughout this time frame.

3. **Calculation:** The VWAP is calculated by dividing the total value of executed trades by the total trading volume during the chosen time period. It provides a benchmark price representing the average price at which the asset traded during that period.

4. **Execution Approach:** VWAP algorithms are passive in nature. They aim to match the pace of trading with the market's natural volume and liquidity, minimizing the disruption of large orders.

5. **Order Slicing:** To achieve the desired execution schedule, the original order is often sliced into smaller portions and executed incrementally. These smaller orders are submitted to the market in a way that approximates the volume distribution of the VWAP.

6. **Benefits:** VWAP strategies are effective for minimizing market impact, especially in assets with high trading volumes. They are commonly used by institutional traders for executing large orders without causing significant price movements.

7. **Challenges:** VWAP strategies may struggle in illiquid markets or during periods of high volatility when order book dynamics change rapidly.

TWAP (Time-Weighted Average Price):

1. **Objective:** TWAP algorithms aim to execute a trading order by evenly distributing it over a specified time period, regardless of trading volume fluctuations. The primary goal is to minimize market impact and achieve an execution price close to the average market price over the entire period.

2. **Time Horizon:** TWAP strategies divide the trading day or a specified time frame into equal intervals and execute portions of the order at regular intervals throughout that period.

3. **Execution Approach:** TWAP algorithms are passive and systematic. They execute orders automatically according to a predetermined schedule, regardless of market conditions.

4. **Benefits:** TWAP strategies are effective for minimizing market impact, especially in assets with stable trading volumes. They are relatively simple to implement and suitable for traders who prefer a consistent execution pace.

5. **Challenges:** TWAP strategies may underperform in highly volatile markets, as they do not adapt to changing liquidity conditions. Traders must carefully choose the time frame and adjust the schedule to suit market dynamics.

Choosing Between VWAP and TWAP:

- **VWAP vs. TWAP:** The choice between VWAP and TWAP depends on the trader's objectives and the asset being traded. VWAP is often preferred when market impact needs to be minimized, especially in high-volume assets. TWAP is suitable when the goal is to execute an order steadily throughout the day with less concern for volume fluctuations.

- **Combination:** Some traders use a combination of VWAP and TWAP strategies, starting with a TWAP in the early part of the trading day and switching to a VWAP in the later part to achieve a balance between consistent execution and minimal market impact.

Ultimately, the choice between VWAP and TWAP, or a combination of both, should align with the trader's specific execution goals, market conditions, and the characteristics of the asset being traded. Additionally, risk management and adaptability are essential factors to consider when implementing these strategies.

Implementation Shortfall and POV (Percentage of Volume) are two commonly used execution algorithms in algorithmic trading. They serve different purposes and are designed to address specific trading objectives. Here's an overview of Implementation Shortfall and POV algorithms:

Implementation Shortfall Algorithm:

Objective:

◈ The Implementation Shortfall (IS) algorithm aims to minimize the difference between the initial target price and the actual execution price of a trading order. It considers historical price movements and market impact to optimize trade execution.

Components of Implementation Shortfall:

1. **Benchmark Price:** The IS algorithm starts with a benchmark price, which is often the price at the time the order is generated.

2. **Real-Time Monitoring:** It continuously monitors market conditions, price movements, and the order's progress.

3. **Execution Decision:** Based on real-time information, the algorithm makes execution decisions to buy or sell, aiming to minimize the cost relative to the benchmark price.

4. **Dynamic Adjustments:** The algorithm may dynamically adjust the order size and execution strategy based on market conditions, liquidity, and historical data.

Execution Process:

◈ The IS algorithm dynamically calculates and updates the cost of the trade as it progresses. It compares the cumulative cost with the initial benchmark price to determine the performance of the trade.

Benefits of Implementation Shortfall:

◈ Effective for minimizing the difference between the expected and actual execution prices.

◈ Takes into account market conditions and historical data to optimize execution.

◈ Suitable for traders concerned about minimizing costs and market impact.

Challenges:

◈ Requires access to real time market data and historical data for accurate performance estimation.

◈ May not be ideal for achieving the best possible price in highly liquid markets.

Percentage of Volume (POV) Algorithm:

Objective:

◈ The Percentage of Volume (POV) algorithm aims to execute a fixed percentage of the total trading volume for an asset within a specified time frame. It adapts to market conditions by adjusting order size.

Components of POV:

1. **Fixed Percentage:** The trader specifies the percentage of the total volume they want to trade within the chosen time frame.

2. **Real-Time Adjustments:** The algorithm continuously monitors trading volume and adjusts the order size to maintain the specified percentage.

3. **Execution Schedule:** It spreads the execution of the order evenly over the specified time frame, ensuring that the targeted percentage is achieved.

Execution Process:

◈ The POV algorithm dynamically calculates the order size based on the current volume, ensuring that the specified percentage is reached by the end of the trading period.

Benefits of Percentage of Volume:

◈ Helps traders achieve a consistent percentage of total trading volume, regardless of market conditions.

◈ Minimizes market impact by distributing the order execution evenly over time.

◈ Allows traders to set clear execution objectives based on volume participation.

Challenges:

◈ May result in varying execution prices, depending on market fluctuations.

◈ May not be suitable for achieving the best possible price in highly volatile or illiquid markets.

Choosing Between IS and POV:

◈ **Implementation Shortfall:** IS is suitable for traders focused on minimizing the difference between the initial benchmark price and the actual execution price. It is especially useful when historical data and real-time monitoring can inform execution decisions.

◈ **Percentage of Volume:** POV is effective for traders who want to participate in a fixed percentage of total volume and maintain a consistent execution schedule. It is often preferred when achieving a specific volume participation target is a priority.

Traders should choose between IS and POV algorithms based on their specific execution goals, asset characteristics, and market conditions. Additionally, some traders may use a combination of execution algorithms to achieve a balance between optimizing execution costs and achieving specific participation targets.

Smart Order Routing (SOR) systems are a critical component of algorithmic trading strategies, especially in multi-market and fragmented trading environments. These systems are designed to automatically route orders to various trading venues (such as stock exchanges, alternative trading systems, and dark pools) in a way that optimizes execution outcomes for the trader. Here's an overview of Smart Order Routing systems:

Objective:

The primary objective of SOR systems is to achieve the best possible execution prices while considering factors like order size, liquidity, market conditions, and trading costs. They aim to minimize the market impact of large orders and efficiently capture available liquidity.

Key Components and Features:

1. **Market Connectivity:** SOR systems are connected to multiple trading venues, providing traders with access to a wide range of liquidity sources. These venues can include public exchanges, dark pools, and off-exchange trading platforms.

2. **Real-Time Data Feeds:** SOR systems rely on real-time market data feeds to continuously assess market conditions, including bid-ask spreads, order book depth, and recent trade prices and volumes.

3. **Order Routing Logic:** SOR algorithms use sophisticated routing logic to determine where and how to route orders. This logic takes into account various factors, including:

� Best execution criteria: SOR systems evaluate which venue is most likely to provide the best execution based on price, liquidity, and trading costs.

� Order size: SOR adjusts the order size based on venue-specific liquidity profiles to minimize market impact.

� Regulatory constraints: Compliance with market regulations and order types is considered in routing decisions.

4. **Order Slicing:** SOR systems often slice large orders into smaller portions to execute incrementally across multiple venues. This minimizes market impact and allows traders to capture liquidity more effectively.

5. **Adaptive Strategies:** Some SOR systems employ adaptive strategies that adjust routing decisions in real-time based on changing market conditions. For example, they may route orders differently during high volatility periods.

6. **Dark Pool Access:** SOR systems may incorporate access to dark pools, which are private trading venues that offer anonymity and seek

to minimize market impact. This allows traders to execute large orders discreetly.

7. **Execution Quality Monitoring:** SOR systems continuously monitor execution quality, comparing actual execution prices to benchmark prices. This helps traders assess the performance of their orders.

Challenges and Considerations:

1. **Market Complexity:** In highly fragmented markets, SOR systems must navigate a complex landscape of trading venues, each with its own rules and characteristics.

2. **Data Latency:** Real-time data latency can impact the speed and accuracy of routing decisions, especially in high-frequency trading.

3. **Regulatory Compliance:** Compliance with regulatory requirements, including best execution obligations, is crucial when designing SOR systems.

4. **Risk Management:** Effective risk management is essential to prevent potential issues, such as erroneous orders or excessive trading.

5. **Venue Relationships:** Developing and maintaining relationships with trading venues is important for ensuring access to liquidity.

Benefits:

◈ SOR systems can help traders achieve better execution prices, reduce trading costs, and minimize market impact.

◈ They provide access to a wide range of liquidity sources, increasing the chances of finding the best execution venues.

◈ SOR systems offer automation and speed, which are crucial for executing orders in rapidly changing markets.

Smart Order Routing (SOR) systems are essential tools for traders, especially in markets with multiple trading venues. They use advanced algorithms and real-time data analysis to intelligently route orders, helping traders achieve their execution objectives while optimizing costs and minimizing market impact.

Chapter 7: Algorithmic Trading in Practice

Real-World Applications of Algorithmic Trading

Algorithmic trading has a wide range of real-world applications across various financial markets and asset classes. Traders and institutions use algorithmic strategies to achieve specific objectives, optimize trade execution, and manage risk. Here are some common real-world applications of algorithmic trading:

1. **Market Making:**

◈ Market makers use algorithmic trading to continuously quote bid and ask prices in the market. They profit from the bid-ask spread and provide liquidity to other market participants.

2. **Statistical Arbitrage:**

◈ Algorithmic trading is employed in statistical arbitrage strategies that involve trading pairs of correlated assets. Algorithms identify deviations from historical price relationships and execute trades to exploit these discrepancies.

3. **Pairs Trading:**

◈ Pairs trading algorithms identify pairs of assets with historical price relationships and execute simultaneous long and short positions to profit from the convergence or divergence of their prices.

4. **Trend Following:**

◈ Trend-following strategies use algorithms to identify and capitalize on trends in asset prices. Algorithms may use technical indicators to determine entry and exit points.

5. **Mean Reversion:**

◈ Mean-reversion algorithms trade based on the belief that asset prices will eventually revert to their historical mean or average. These strategies aim to profit from price reversals.

6. **High-Frequency Trading (HFT):**

◈ High-frequency trading firms use extremely fast algorithms to execute a large number of trades in milliseconds or microseconds. HFT strategies focus on capturing small price discrepancies and liquidity imbalances.

7. **Execution Algorithms:**

◈ Execution algorithms, such as VWAP and TWAP, are widely used to execute large orders efficiently and minimize market impact. These algorithms are particularly important for institutional traders.

8. **Smart Order Routing (SOR):**

◈ SOR algorithms automatically route orders to various trading venues to obtain the best execution prices. They consider factors like order size, liquidity, and market conditions.

9. **Arbitrage Opportunities:**

◈ Arbitrage algorithms exploit price differences between different markets or exchanges. For example, arbitrageurs may trade the same asset on multiple exchanges to profit from price disparities.

10. **Options Market Making:**

◈ Market makers in options markets use algorithmic strategies to manage their options portfolios, quote options prices, and hedge their positions.

11. **Forex (Foreign Exchange) Trading:**

◈ Algorithmic trading is prevalent in the forex market, where algorithms execute currency trades based on technical indicators, economic data releases, and market sentiment.

12. **Commodity Trading:**

◈ Algorithms are used in commodity markets for trading futures contracts, managing commodity portfolios, and hedging against price fluctuations.

13. **Fixed Income Trading:**

◈ In the fixed income market, algorithmic trading strategies help optimize bond and fixed income portfolio management, particularly for large institutional investors.

14. **Crypto Trading:**

◈ Algorithmic trading is becoming increasingly popular in cryptocurrency markets, where traders use algorithms to execute trades across various digital assets and exchanges.

15. **Risk Management:**

◈ Algorithms are used to manage risk by automatically adjusting portfolio positions, implementing stop-loss orders, and hedging against adverse market movements.

16. **Machine Learning-Based Trading:**

◈ Machine learning and artificial intelligence are applied to develop trading algorithms that can adapt to changing market conditions, identify patterns, and make predictions.

These real-world applications of algorithmic trading demonstrate its versatility and adaptability across different financial markets and trading strategies. Traders and financial institutions continually innovate and develop new algorithmic approaches to meet their specific trading goals and navigate the complexities of modern financial markets.

Algorithmic trading in equity markets is a prevalent and sophisticated practice that involves the use of computer algorithms to execute buy or sell orders for stocks and other equity-related securities. These algorithms are designed to optimize trade execution, minimize market impact, and capitalize on various trading strategies. Here's an overview of algorithmic trading in equity markets:

Key Components and Aspects of Algorithmic Trading in Equity Markets:

1. **Order Types:** Algorithmic traders can use various order types, including market orders, limit orders, stop orders, and more, depending on their trading objectives and strategies.

2. **Trading Strategies:** Algorithmic trading in equity markets encompasses a wide range of strategies, such as market making, statistical arbitrage, pairs trading, trend following, and mean reversion.

3. **Liquidity Analysis:** Algorithms often analyze liquidity and order book depth to determine the best venues and times to execute orders without causing significant price fluctuations.

4. **Risk Management:** Effective risk management is crucial in equity algorithmic trading. Risk controls, such as position limits and stop-loss mechanisms, help mitigate potential losses.

5. **Market Data:** Real-time market data feeds are essential for algorithmic trading. These feeds provide information on stock prices, trading volumes, order book depth, and trade execution data.

6. **Execution Algorithms:** Various execution algorithms are used in equity markets, including VWAP, TWAP, IS, POV, and smart order routing (SOR) algorithms. These algorithms are selected based on the specific execution objectives of the trader.

7. **Latency and Speed:** Low latency is critical for algorithmic trading in equity markets, especially in high-frequency trading (HFT). Faster execution can provide a competitive advantage.

8. **Market Microstructure:** Understanding the market microstructure of equity markets, including order types, bid-ask spreads, and market participants, is essential for effective algorithmic trading.

9. **Regulatory Compliance:** Traders must adhere to regulatory requirements, such as best execution standards and reporting obligations, when conducting algorithmic trading in equity markets.

Common Algorithmic Trading Strategies in Equity Markets:

1. **Market Making:** Market makers provide continuous bid and ask quotes in the market, profiting from the bid-ask spread. Algorithms are used to manage market-making positions and adapt to changing market conditions.

2. **Statistical Arbitrage:** Statistical arbitrage strategies involve trading pairs of stocks based on statistical relationships and historical correlations. Algorithms identify deviations from historical patterns to execute trades.

3. **Pairs Trading:** Pairs trading algorithms identify pairs of correlated stocks and execute long and short positions simultaneously, profiting from the convergence or divergence of their prices.

4. **Trend Following:** Trend-following algorithms identify and exploit trends in stock prices. They may use technical indicators to determine entry and exit points.

5. **Mean Reversion:** Mean-reversion algorithms trade based on the belief that stock prices will eventually revert to their historical means or averages. These strategies aim to profit from price reversals.

6. **High-Frequency Trading (HFT):** HFT firms use ultra-fast algorithms to execute a large number of trades in milliseconds or microseconds. HFT strategies focus on capturing small price discrepancies and liquidity imbalances.

7. **Smart Order Routing (SOR):** SOR algorithms automatically route orders to various trading venues to obtain the best execution prices. They consider factors like order size, liquidity, and market conditions.

8. **Dark Pool Access:** Algorithms may route orders to dark pools, which are private trading venues, to execute large orders away from public exchanges, reducing market impact.

9. **Machine Learning-Based Trading:** Machine learning and AI algorithms are applied to develop trading strategies that can adapt to changing market conditions and make predictions based on large datasets.

Algorithmic trading has become a fundamental part of equity markets, with the ability to provide liquidity, enhance market efficiency, and execute complex strategies at high speeds. Traders and institutions continue to invest in technology and research to develop advanced algorithms and gain a competitive edge in these markets.

Algorithmic trading is not limited to equity markets; it is also extensively used in fixed income and foreign exchange (FX) markets. In these markets, algorithmic trading serves various purposes, including optimizing execution, managing risk, and implementing trading strategies. Here's an overview of algorithmic trading in fixed income and FX markets:

Algorithmic Trading in Fixed Income Markets:

1. **Fixed Income Instruments:** Fixed income markets involve a wide range of instruments, such as government bonds, corporate bonds, municipal bonds, and mortgage-backed securities.

2. **Execution Algorithms:** Algorithmic trading in fixed income markets employs execution algorithms similar to those in equity markets, including VWAP, TWAP, IS, and others. These algorithms aim to efficiently execute large bond orders while minimizing market impact.

3. **Liquidity Analysis:** Algorithms analyze the liquidity of different bond issues and maturities to determine the best venues and times for execution. Fixed income markets can be less liquid than equity markets, making liquidity analysis crucial.

4. **Risk Management:** Risk management is a top priority in fixed income algorithmic trading due to the potential illiquidity of certain bonds and interest rate fluctuations. Algorithms often incorporate risk controls, position limits, and duration management.

5. **Market Data:** Real-time market data is essential for fixed income algorithmic trading. Traders rely on data sources that provide information on bond prices, yields, credit spreads, and economic indicators.

6. **Regulatory Compliance:** Compliance with regulations, including best execution standards, reporting requirements, and trade transparency rules, is essential for fixed income algorithmic trading.

Algorithmic Trading in FX Markets:

1. **Currency Pairs:** In the FX market, algorithmic trading involves trading currency pairs, such as EUR/USD, USD/JPY, and GBP/USD. FX markets are known for their high liquidity and 24-hour trading.

2. **Execution Algorithms:** FX algorithmic trading uses execution algorithms like VWAP, TWAP, and IS, similar to other asset classes. These algorithms aim to execute currency trades efficiently and at favorable exchange rates.

3. **High Liquidity:** FX markets are highly liquid, making it possible to execute large orders without significant price impact. Algorithms in the FX market focus on optimizing execution costs.

4. **Arbitrage Opportunities:** FX algorithms can exploit arbitrage opportunities arising from price discrepancies between different currency pairs or exchanges. Triangular arbitrage and statistical arbitrage are common FX strategies.

5. **Hedging:** Many corporations and financial institutions use algorithmic trading to hedge currency exposure. Algorithms execute hedging strategies based on market movements and the institution's risk profile.

6. **Machine Learning-Based Trading:** Machine learning and AI algorithms are increasingly applied to FX trading. These algorithms can analyze vast amounts of data, identify patterns, and make predictive currency exchange rate forecasts.

7. **Algorithmic Options Trading:** In the FX options market, algorithms are used for options pricing, volatility modeling, and options strategies such as straddles and strangles.

Benefits of Algorithmic Trading in Fixed Income and FX Markets:

◈ Improved trade execution: Algorithms help traders achieve better execution prices and reduce transaction costs.

◈ Risk management: Algorithms manage risk by implementing stop-loss orders, adjusting positions, and hedging currency or interest rate exposure.

◈ Liquidity access: Algorithms in these markets provide access to liquidity sources and optimize order routing to reduce market impact.

◈ Efficiency: Algorithmic trading allows for efficient execution of complex trading strategies across multiple instruments and markets.

◈ Automation: Automation reduces manual trading effort and human error, especially in FX markets that operate 24/5.

Algorithmic trading has a significant presence in fixed income and FX markets. Traders in these markets leverage algorithmic strategies to enhance execution, manage risk, and implement a wide range of trading strategies. With the continued evolution of technology and data analytics, algorithmic trading is expected to play an increasingly important role in these asset classes.

Algorithmic trading has gained significant popularity in the cryptocurrency markets due to the high volatility and 24/7 trading availability in the crypto space. Traders and institutions use algorithms to execute various strategies, manage risk, and take advantage of price fluctuations in cryptocurrencies. Here's an overview of algorithmic trading in cryptocurrencies:

Key Aspects of Algorithmic Trading in Cryptocurrencies:

1. **Cryptocurrency Market Diversity:** Cryptocurrency markets offer a wide range of digital assets, including Bitcoin (BTC), Ethereum (ETH), Ripple (XRP), and numerous altcoins. Algorithmic traders can apply strategies to individual cryptocurrencies or create portfolios of multiple assets.

2. **24/7 Trading:** Cryptocurrency markets operate 24/7, allowing algorithmic traders to execute strategies at any time, including weekends and holidays.

3. **High Volatility:** Cryptocurrencies are known for their price volatility, providing opportunities for profit through rapid price movements. Algorithmic strategies can capitalize on these price fluctuations.

4. **Liquidity Variability:** Liquidity can vary significantly among cryptocurrencies. Some, like Bitcoin, have high liquidity, while others may have lower trading volumes. Algorithms assess liquidity and adapt strategies accordingly.

5. **Exchange Diversity:** Cryptocurrencies are traded on numerous cryptocurrency exchanges worldwide. Algorithmic traders often employ smart order routing (SOR) to access different exchanges and optimize execution.

6. **Market Microstructure:** Understanding the microstructure of cryptocurrency markets, including order book dynamics, order types, and exchange mechanics, is crucial for algorithmic trading success.

7. **Execution Algorithms:** Execution algorithms like VWAP, TWAP, and IS are adapted for cryptocurrency trading to achieve efficient execution while minimizing market impact.

8. **Risk Management:** Risk management is vital in cryptocurrency trading due to the high volatility. Algorithms may incorporate stop-loss orders, position sizing, and risk limits to protect capital.

Common Algorithmic Trading Strategies in Cryptocurrencies:

1. **Market Making:** Market makers provide liquidity by continuously quoting bid and ask prices on cryptocurrency exchanges. Algorithms manage the order book and profit from the bid-ask spread.

2. **Arbitrage:** Cryptocurrency arbitrage strategies involve buying an asset on one exchange where it's priced lower and selling it on another exchange where it's priced higher. Algorithms identify arbitrage opportunities and execute trades.

3. **Trend Following:** Trend-following algorithms analyze historical price data and indicators to identify and capitalize on upward or downward trends in cryptocurrency prices.

4. **Mean Reversion:** Mean-reversion strategies aim to profit from the belief that cryptocurrency prices will revert to their historical averages. Algorithms identify overbought or oversold conditions and execute trades accordingly.

5. **Statistical Arbitrage:** Statistical arbitrage strategies involve trading pairs of correlated cryptocurrencies. Algorithms identify deviations from historical correlations and execute trades when the correlation is expected to revert.

6. **Quantitative Strategies:** Algorithmic traders may use quantitative models to make predictions about cryptocurrency prices based on various factors, including market sentiment, news sentiment, and fundamental data.

7. **Machine Learning-Based Strategies:** Machine learning and artificial intelligence are applied to analyze vast amounts of cryptocurrency data and make trading decisions based on patterns and predictions.

Benefits of Algorithmic Trading in Cryptocurrencies:

◈ Efficient execution: Algorithms can execute trades quickly and efficiently across multiple cryptocurrency exchanges.

◈ Liquidity provision: Market-making algorithms help maintain liquidity in cryptocurrency markets.

◈ Risk management: Algorithms assist in managing risk by automating risk control measures.

◈ Diversification: Algorithmic traders can diversify their portfolios by trading multiple cryptocurrencies simultaneously.

◈ Round-the-clock trading: Algorithmic strategies can operate 24/7 to take advantage of cryptocurrency market movements at any time.

Algorithmic trading has become an integral part of the cryptocurrency ecosystem, catering to both individual and institutional traders. As the cryptocurrency market continues to evolve, algorithmic strategies are expected to adapt and develop further to meet the growing demand for efficient trading and risk management solutions.

Chapter 8: Risk Management and Compliance

Risk Assessment and Mitigation in Algorithmic Trading

Effective risk management is a critical component of algorithmic trading. Algorithmic traders face various types of risks, including market risk, execution risk, operational risk, and regulatory compliance risk. To ensure the stability and success of algorithmic trading strategies, traders and institutions must conduct thorough risk assessments and implement risk mitigation measures. Here's an overview of risk assessment and mitigation in algorithmic trading:

1. Market Risk:

◈ **Definition:** Market risk is the potential for financial losses due to adverse market movements, such as price fluctuations, volatility, and adverse market events.

◈ **Risk Assessment:** Traders assess market risk by analyzing historical price data, volatility measures, and potential adverse scenarios that could affect their trading strategies.

◈ **Risk Mitigation:** Strategies for mitigating market risk include portfolio diversification, stop-loss orders, and hedging strategies. Risk models and stress tests can help traders understand potential losses under extreme market conditions.

2. Execution Risk:

◈ **Definition:** Execution risk refers to the potential for losses due to difficulties in executing trades as intended, including issues related to order routing and market impact.

◈ **Risk Assessment:** Traders assess execution risk by monitoring the performance of execution algorithms, analyzing slippage, and evaluating the effectiveness of smart order routing.

◈ **Risk Mitigation:** Mitigating execution risk involves using effective execution algorithms, setting order size limits, and regularly reviewing and optimizing trading strategies. Traders may also use backup execution strategies in case of algorithm failure.

3. Operational Risk:

◈ **Definition:** Operational risk includes risks related to technology failures, system glitches, human errors, and other operational issues that can disrupt trading activities.

◈ **Risk Assessment:** Traders assess operational risk by conducting regular system audits, monitoring system uptime, and analyzing historical incidents.

◈ **Risk Mitigation:** To mitigate operational risk, traders invest in robust infrastructure, implement redundancy measures, and establish disaster recovery plans. Comprehensive testing and monitoring of systems and processes are crucial for identifying and addressing operational vulnerabilities.

4. Regulatory Compliance Risk:

◈ **Definition:** Regulatory compliance risk arises from failing to adhere to relevant financial regulations and industry standards.

◈ **Risk Assessment:** Traders assess compliance risk by staying informed about evolving regulations, conducting compliance audits, and ensuring that algorithms and trading practices adhere to regulatory requirements.

◈ **Risk Mitigation:** Compliance risk can be mitigated by implementing robust compliance programs, maintaining accurate records, and staying up-to-date with regulatory changes. Collaboration with legal and compliance experts is essential to ensure adherence to rules and regulations.

5. Model Risk:

◈ **Definition:** Model risk occurs when the trading algorithm's assumptions or parameters are incorrect, leading to unexpected losses.

◈ **Risk Assessment:** Traders assess model risk by conducting rigorous testing and validation of algorithmic models, including sensitivity analysis and backtesting.

◈ **Risk Mitigation:** Model risk can be mitigated by continuously monitoring and updating trading models, using multiple models for decision-making, and implementing model validation processes.

6. Liquidity Risk:

◈ **Definition:** Liquidity risk is the risk of being unable to execute trades at desired prices due to insufficient market liquidity.

◈ **Risk Assessment:** Traders assess liquidity risk by analyzing order book depth, historical liquidity patterns, and market conditions.

◈ **Risk Mitigation:** Mitigating liquidity risk involves using algorithms that adapt to changing liquidity conditions, optimizing order placement strategies, and setting realistic order execution expectations.

7. Counterparty Risk:

◈ **Definition:** Counterparty risk arises from the potential failure of a trading counterparty or exchange, leading to financial losses.

◈ **Risk Assessment:** Traders assess counterparty risk by evaluating the financial stability and reputation of trading counterparties and exchanges.

◈ **Risk Mitigation:** Counterparty risk can be mitigated by using reputable and regulated counterparties and implementing collateral and risk management procedures.

Effective risk assessment and mitigation are essential for the long-term success of algorithmic trading strategies. Traders and institutions must proactively identify, monitor, and manage risks to protect capital and ensure compliance with regulatory requirements. A well-structured risk management framework helps algorithmic traders navigate the complexities of modern financial markets while safeguarding their interests.

The regulatory framework for algorithmic traders varies by country and region, with different regulatory bodies overseeing financial markets and trading activities. The regulations governing algorithmic trading are designed to promote market integrity, protect investors, and ensure fair and orderly trading. Here's an overview of the regulatory framework for algorithmic traders:

1. Securities and Exchange Commission (SEC) - United States:

◈ The SEC regulates securities markets in the United States and imposes rules on algorithmic trading activities.

◈ Key regulations include Regulation NMS, which addresses market structure and fair access, and Rule 15c3-5, known as the Market Access Rule, which requires broker-dealers to establish risk controls for algorithmic trading.

2. Commodity Futures Trading Commission (CFTC) - United States:

◈ The CFTC regulates futures and derivatives markets in the United States, including algorithmic trading activities.

◈ Regulations such as Rule 1.73 require pre-trade risk controls for algorithmic trading in futures markets.

3. European Securities and Markets Authority (ESMA) - European Union:

◈ ESMA oversees securities markets in the European Union (EU) and has issued directives and regulations that impact algorithmic trading, including MiFID II (Markets in Financial Instruments Directive II).

◈ MiFID II introduced requirements for algorithmic trading, including reporting obligations, transparency requirements, and market access controls.

4. Financial Conduct Authority (FCA) - United Kingdom:

◈ The FCA regulates financial markets in the UK and has specific rules and guidance on algorithmic trading.

◈ The FCA's Market Conduct Sourcebook (MAR) includes regulations related to algorithmic trading, including order handling and systems and controls requirements.

5. Securities and Futures Commission (SFC) - Hong Kong:

◈ The SFC regulates securities and futures markets in Hong Kong, and it has issued guidelines and requirements for algorithmic trading.

◈ Algorithmic traders in Hong Kong are subject to the SFC's Code of Conduct for Persons Licensed by or Registered with the SFC.

6. Monetary Authority of Singapore (MAS) - Singapore:

◈ The MAS regulates financial markets in Singapore and has established rules and guidelines for algorithmic trading activities.

◈ The MAS's Guidelines on Electronic Trading provide guidance on risk management, system controls, and market access for algorithmic traders.

7. Japan Financial Services Agency (FSA) - Japan:

◈ The FSA oversees financial markets in Japan and has introduced regulations related to algorithmic trading.

◈ Algorithmic traders in Japan are subject to the Financial Instruments and Exchange Act (FIEA), which includes rules on order cancellation, market access, and risk management.

8. Other Regional Regulators:

◈ Many other countries and regions have their own regulatory authorities that oversee algorithmic trading activities. These regulators may have specific rules and reporting requirements for algorithmic traders operating within their jurisdictions.

Key Regulatory Considerations for Algorithmic Traders:

◈ **Risk Controls:** Regulators often require algorithmic traders to implement pre-trade risk controls, such as circuit breakers, position limits, and kill switches, to manage the risk of erroneous or disruptive trading.

◈ **Market Access:** Regulations may govern how algorithmic traders access and interact with trading venues, including rules for order placement, cancellation, and modification.

◈ **Reporting and Record-Keeping:** Regulators typically require algorithmic traders to maintain records of their trading activities and report certain trading data, including large trades and suspicious activity.

◈ **Market Manipulation and Abuse:** Regulators have strict rules against market manipulation and abusive trading practices, and algorithmic traders must adhere to these rules.

◈ **Cybersecurity and System Resilience:** Regulatory authorities emphasize the importance of robust cybersecurity measures and system resilience to protect against cyber threats and system failures.

It's essential for algorithmic traders to stay informed about the regulatory requirements in their respective jurisdictions and comply with applicable rules and guidelines. Compliance with regulatory standards not only helps traders avoid legal and financial consequences but also contributes to the overall integrity and stability of financial markets.

Algorithmic trading ethics and compliance are crucial considerations for traders and financial institutions engaged in automated trading activities. Ethical behavior and compliance with regulatory standards help maintain market integrity, protect investors, and ensure fair and transparent trading practices. Here are key aspects of algorithmic trading ethics and compliance:

1. Fair and Ethical Trading Practices:

◈ Algorithmic traders should adhere to principles of fairness and ethics in their trading activities. This includes refraining from engaging in manipulative or deceptive practices that could harm market integrity or investors.

2. Regulatory Compliance:

⟐ Compliance with applicable financial regulations and market rules is paramount. Traders and institutions must be aware of and adhere to the rules and guidelines set forth by regulatory authorities in their respective jurisdictions.

3. Best Execution:

⟐ Algorithmic traders have a duty to seek best execution for their clients or funds. This means striving to achieve the most favorable terms for trade execution, considering factors like price, speed, cost, and likelihood of execution.

4. Risk Management:

⟐ Effective risk management is a key ethical consideration. Traders must implement risk controls and risk mitigation measures to protect against potential losses, system failures, and adverse market conditions.

5. Transparency and Disclosure:

⟐ Algorithmic traders should provide clear and accurate information to clients and counterparties regarding their trading strategies, practices, and potential conflicts of interest. Transparency builds trust in the market.

6. Data Privacy and Security:

⟐ Safeguarding sensitive data and client information is essential. Traders must comply with data privacy regulations and implement robust cybersecurity measures to protect against data breaches and cyber threats.

7. Anti-Money Laundering (AML) and Know Your Customer (KYC):

◈ Compliance with AML and KYC regulations is essential to prevent illegal activities, such as money laundering and terrorist financing, from occurring through algorithmic trading.

8. Market Manipulation and Abuse:

◈ Traders must avoid engaging in market manipulation or abusive trading practices. This includes practices like spoofing, layering, and wash trading, which are strictly prohibited by regulators.

9. System Resilience and Contingency Planning:

◈ Maintaining system resilience and implementing contingency plans are ethical obligations. Algorithmic traders should be prepared for system failures and disruptions, ensuring that they do not adversely affect market stability.

10. Monitoring and Compliance Oversight:

◈ Establishing monitoring mechanisms and compliance oversight is crucial. Internal controls, audits, and compliance officers play a role in ensuring that algorithmic trading practices remain ethical and compliant.

11. Training and Education:

◈ Traders and their staff should receive proper training and education on ethical and compliance standards. This helps promote a culture of ethics and compliance within the organization.

12. Accountability and Reporting:

◈ Algorithmic traders should hold individuals and teams accountable for ethical and compliance breaches. Reporting mechanisms should be in place to address and rectify any violations promptly.

Ethical algorithmic trading is not only a legal requirement but also a matter of reputation and trust within the financial industry. Violations of ethical standards and regulatory compliance can result in legal consequences, financial penalties, reputational damage, and loss of client trust. To maintain a strong ethical and compliant foundation, traders and institutions should stay informed about regulatory developments, regularly update their internal policies and procedures, and prioritize ethical behavior in their trading activities.

Algorithmic trading, while offering many advantages, can also lead to significant failures and costly consequences when not properly managed or when systems malfunction. Here are a few notable case studies on algorithmic trading failures:

1. Knight Capital Group (2012):

◈ In August 2012, Knight Capital Group, a major market maker in the U.S. equity markets, experienced a catastrophic algorithmic trading failure. A software glitch in one of their trading algorithms caused the firm to execute a large number of erroneous orders in just 45 minutes.

◈ The glitch led to a massive loss of approximately $440 million in a single trading day, almost causing the firm to go bankrupt. Knight Capital was eventually acquired by Virtu Financial to prevent its collapse.

2. Flash Crash (2010):

◈ The Flash Crash of May 6, 2010, is one of the most infamous events in modern financial history. It involved a sudden and severe market crash, where the Dow Jones Industrial Average plummeted by nearly 1,000 points in minutes, only to recover shortly afterward.

◈ While the Flash Crash had multiple causes, including macroeconomic factors, a significant contributing factor was the prevalence of high-frequency trading algorithms that exacerbated the rapid market movements.

3. BNY Mellon (2015):

◈ In 2015, BNY Mellon faced regulatory scrutiny and penalties related to its foreign exchange trading practices. The bank was accused of providing improper pricing to its customers in foreign exchange transactions conducted through its standing instruction program, which relied on algorithmic pricing.

◈ BNY Mellon agreed to pay $714 million in fines and restitution to settle the charges.

4. EBS (2016):

◈ In January 2016, the EBS foreign exchange trading platform, operated by ICAP, experienced a technical glitch. The malfunction disrupted trading on the platform and led to a halt in trading for several hours.

◈ The incident affected currency markets, as EBS is one of the largest electronic foreign exchange platforms globally.

5. Deutsche Bank (2016):

◈ In 2016, Deutsche Bank faced regulatory action for its failure to maintain adequate risk controls and supervision over its equities trading platform. The bank's algorithms were found to have engaged in millions of erroneous options trades.

◈ Deutsche Bank agreed to pay a $9.5 million penalty to settle the charges.

These case studies highlight the potential risks associated with algorithmic trading, including software glitches, inadequate risk controls, and unintended consequences. They underscore the importance of robust risk management, thorough testing, and compliance with regulatory standards in algorithmic trading activities. Financial institutions have since redoubled their efforts to prevent such failures and enhance the resilience of their algorithmic trading systems.

Chapter 9: Advanced Topics in Algorithmic Trading

Machine Learning and Artificial Intelligence in Trading

Machine learning (ML) and artificial intelligence (AI) have transformed the landscape of algorithmic trading. These advanced technologies offer powerful tools for data analysis, prediction, and strategy development. Here's an exploration of how ML and AI are applied in trading:

1. Predictive Modeling:

◈ ML algorithms can analyze historical price data, order book data, and various market indicators to make predictions about future price movements. This is particularly useful in developing trend-following and mean-reversion strategies.

2. Sentiment Analysis:

◈ Natural language processing (NLP) and sentiment analysis techniques are used to assess news articles, social media feeds, and other textual data sources. This can help traders gauge market sentiment and make informed trading decisions.

3. Pattern Recognition:

◈ ML algorithms excel at identifying complex patterns in data. In trading, this is used for recognizing chart patterns, candlestick patterns, and other technical analysis signals.

4. Algorithmic Portfolio Management:

◈ AI-driven algorithms can optimize portfolio construction, taking into account risk tolerance, diversification, and return objectives. They rebalance portfolios dynamically based on changing market conditions.

5. Market Microstructure Analysis:

◈ ML models can analyze market microstructure data to gain insights into order flow, order book dynamics, and liquidity patterns. This information helps traders optimize execution strategies.

6. High-Frequency Trading (HFT):

◈ HFT firms employ ML and AI to develop lightning-fast algorithms that can analyze and execute trades in microseconds. These algorithms focus on capturing small price discrepancies and liquidity imbalances.

7. Risk Management:

◈ ML models assess portfolio risk by simulating various market scenarios and estimating potential losses. They can also trigger risk control mechanisms, such as stop-loss orders.

8. Algorithmic Options Trading:

◈ AI algorithms are applied to options pricing, volatility modeling, and the development of options trading strategies, such as straddles and strangles.

9. Deep Learning:

◈ Deep learning techniques, a subset of ML, have shown promise in developing predictive models for algorithmic trading. Deep neural networks can capture intricate patterns in large datasets.

10. Reinforcement Learning: - Reinforcement learning algorithms can adapt trading strategies based on rewards and penalties, learning from both historical data and real-time interactions with the market.

11. Algorithmic Risk Assessment: - ML models can analyze trading patterns and historical data to detect potential fraudulent or manipulative trading activities.

12. Automation and Robo-Advisors: - AI-driven robo-advisors use ML to manage portfolios, make investment decisions, and offer personalized financial advice to retail investors.

13. Market Making and Liquidity Provision: - ML algorithms are used by market makers to optimize quotes and manage positions. These algorithms continuously adapt to changing market conditions.

While ML and AI offer immense potential in algorithmic trading, they also come with challenges, including data quality, model interpretability, and overfitting. Additionally, the rapid advancement of these technologies necessitates ongoing research and development to stay competitive in the trading industry. As a result, algorithmic trading firms and financial institutions continue to invest in ML and AI to gain a competitive edge in the ever-evolving financial markets.

High-frequency trading (HFT) strategies are a subset of algorithmic trading strategies that involve the rapid execution of a large number of trades in a very short period, often measured in milliseconds or microseconds. HFT firms leverage advanced technology, ultra-fast computer systems, and sophisticated algorithms to capitalize on small price discrepancies, market inefficiencies, and liquidity imbalances. Here are some common HFT strategies:

1. **Market Making:** HFT firms act as market makers by continuously quoting bid and ask prices for securities. They profit from the bid-ask spread—the difference between the buying (bid) and selling (ask) prices. Market makers provide liquidity to the market and help maintain price stability.

2. **Arbitrage Strategies:**

◈ **Statistical Arbitrage:** HFT firms use statistical models to identify and trade securities that have historically correlated but have deviated from their expected relationship. When the correlation reverts, the HFT firm profits.

◈ **Triangular Arbitrage:** In the foreign exchange market, HFT algorithms exploit price discrepancies between three currency pairs to profit from arbitrage opportunities.

3. **Trend Following:** HFT firms use technical indicators, price patterns, and historical data to identify short-term trends in asset prices. They then execute trades in the direction of the trend, aiming to profit from momentum.

4. **Mean Reversion:** HFT strategies based on mean reversion take advantage of the belief that asset prices will revert to their historical averages. Algorithms identify overbought or oversold conditions and execute trades expecting a return to the mean.

5. **Pairs Trading:** HFT firms employ pairs trading strategies that involve trading pairs of correlated assets. When the spread between the assets in the pair widens or narrows significantly, the HFT algorithm initiates long and short positions to profit from the convergence or divergence of their prices.

6. **Liquidity Provision:** HFT algorithms monitor order book depth and trading activity to identify moments of high volatility or market imbalance. They then provide liquidity by placing and removing orders strategically to profit from price fluctuations.

7. **News and Event-Based Trading:** HFT algorithms analyze news feeds and economic data releases to make rapid trading decisions based on the information's impact on asset prices. These algorithms can execute trades within microseconds of a news release.

8. **Machine Learning-Based Strategies:** Some HFT firms use machine learning models to develop trading strategies that adapt to changing market conditions and make predictions based on large datasets. These strategies can include sentiment analysis and pattern recognition.

9. **Market Fragmentation Strategies:** HFT firms leverage smart order routing (SOR) algorithms to route orders to multiple trading venues, including stock exchanges and dark pools, to seek the best execution prices and liquidity.

10. **Market-Making in Options:** HFT firms engage in high-speed market-making activities in options markets, continuously quoting option prices and adjusting them based on market conditions.

11. **Spoofing and Layering Detection:** HFT firms often employ algorithms to detect and report spoofing and layering activities that manipulate market prices.

It's important to note that HFT is a highly competitive field where speed and technology infrastructure are critical. HFT firms invest heavily in cutting-edge hardware, low-latency data feeds, and co-location services to gain an advantage in executing trades faster than competitors. However, this level of competition has led to concerns about market stability and the potential for disruptive events, prompting regulatory scrutiny in some cases. As a result, regulations and market structure have evolved to address these challenges in high-frequency trading.

Algorithmic trading is widely used in options and derivatives markets, where complex instruments and strategies require sophisticated automation and execution. Here's an overview of algorithmic trading in options and derivatives:

1. Liquidity Provision:

◈ Market makers in options and derivatives employ algorithmic strategies to provide continuous liquidity. These algorithms continuously update quotes for various options and futures contracts, narrowing spreads, and improving market efficiency.

2. Delta Hedging:

◈ Delta hedging strategies involve dynamically adjusting the underlying positions of options to maintain a delta-neutral portfolio. Algorithms monitor market movements and execute trades to offset delta exposure, reducing risk.

3. Volatility Trading:

◈ Algorithms in options and derivatives markets can execute strategies based on expected changes in volatility. For example, they may buy or sell options straddles or strangles in anticipation of increased price volatility.

4. Statistical Arbitrage:

◈ Statistical arbitrage strategies are used in derivatives trading to exploit price discrepancies between related instruments, such as futures and options on the same underlying asset. Algorithms identify deviations from historical correlations and execute trades when prices are expected to converge.

5. Implied Volatility Trading:

◈ Algorithms analyze implied volatility levels in options markets and execute trades based on perceived mispricings. Traders use statistical models to determine whether implied volatility is overvalued or undervalued relative to historical volatility.

6. Options Spreading:

◈ Spreading strategies involve trading multiple options contracts simultaneously, aiming to profit from the price relationship between them. Algorithms can execute complex spread strategies efficiently.

7. Risk Management:

◈ Algorithms in options and derivatives trading continuously monitor risk exposure and execute hedging trades to manage risk. This includes dynamically adjusting positions and rebalancing portfolios based on market movements.

8. Multi-Leg Strategies:

◈ Multi-leg options strategies, such as iron condors, butterflies, and calendar spreads, are executed using algorithms. These strategies involve simultaneous positions in multiple options contracts with different strike prices and expiration dates.

9. Machine Learning and Complex Models:

◈ Advanced machine learning models are applied to analyze large datasets and identify patterns in options and derivatives markets. These models can assist in predicting price movements, implied volatility changes, and market trends.

10. Market Access and Execution Algorithms: - Algorithms are used to optimize order routing and execution across various options and derivatives exchanges. This includes assessing the liquidity of different venues and selecting the most suitable execution paths.

11. Regulatory Compliance: - Compliance with regulatory requirements, such as position limits and reporting obligations, is a critical aspect of algorithmic trading in options and derivatives. Algorithms must ensure that trading activities adhere to relevant regulations.

12. High-Frequency Trading (HFT): - HFT firms engage in high-speed trading of options and derivatives, seeking to exploit small price discrepancies and market inefficiencies. They often employ ultra-fast algorithms and infrastructure to execute trades within microseconds.

Options and derivatives markets are known for their complexity, and algorithmic trading plays a significant role in providing liquidity, managing risk, and implementing a wide range of trading strategies in these asset classes. As these markets continue to evolve and expand, algorithmic traders leverage increasingly sophisticated technologies and data analysis techniques to gain a competitive edge.

Algorithmic trading is at the core of many quantitative hedge funds' strategies. These funds rely on advanced mathematical and statistical models, as well as automated trading algorithms, to identify trading opportunities, manage risk, and generate returns. Here's an overview of algorithmic trading in quantitative hedge funds:

1. Quantitative Research and Model Development:

� Quantitative hedge funds employ teams of quantitative analysts (quants) who develop mathematical models and trading strategies. These models often use historical data, statistical analysis, and machine learning to identify patterns and relationships in financial markets.

2. Alpha Generation:

� The primary goal of quantitative strategies is to generate alpha, which represents the excess return earned by a hedge fund above a specified benchmark or risk-free rate. Alpha can be derived from factors such as statistical arbitrage, mean reversion, or trend-following signals.

3. Trading Algorithm Development:

◈ Quantitative hedge funds create proprietary trading algorithms to execute their strategies. These algorithms are designed to handle various asset classes, including equities, fixed income, currencies, and derivatives.

4. High-Frequency Trading (HFT):

◈ Some quantitative hedge funds engage in high-frequency trading, where they execute a large number of orders at incredibly high speeds. HFT strategies aim to profit from small price discrepancies and liquidity imbalances in the market.

5. Risk Management:

◈ Risk management is a critical component of quantitative trading. Hedge funds use algorithms to monitor and manage risk exposure, including value-at-risk (VaR) calculations, stop-loss orders, and position sizing algorithms.

6. Market Microstructure Analysis:

◈ Quantitative strategies often incorporate market microstructure analysis to understand order book dynamics, liquidity patterns, and market impact. This helps optimize execution algorithms and minimize transaction costs.

7. Machine Learning and AI:

◈ Many quantitative hedge funds leverage machine learning and artificial intelligence to enhance their models and algorithms. These technologies can analyze vast datasets, identify nonlinear relationships, and adapt to changing market conditions.

8. Portfolio Optimization:

◈ Algorithms are used to construct and manage portfolios of assets. These algorithms consider risk factors, correlations, and return expectations to optimize portfolio weights.

9. Statistical Arbitrage:

◈ Statistical arbitrage strategies involve identifying and exploiting short-term deviations from statistical relationships between assets. Quantitative models assess the likelihood of these deviations reverting, allowing for profitable trading opportunities.

10. Pairs Trading: - Pairs trading strategies are popular among quantitative hedge funds. Algorithms identify pairs of assets with historically correlated price movements and execute trades when the correlation deviates from the norm.

11. Event-Driven Strategies: - Algorithms in quantitative funds can process news and event data to identify trading opportunities based on events like earnings releases, economic announcements, or geopolitical developments.

12. Execution Algorithms: - Hedge funds use execution algorithms to optimize the timing and pricing of their trades. These algorithms aim to minimize market impact, slippage, and transaction costs.

13. Regulatory Compliance: - Hedge funds must ensure that their algorithmic trading activities comply with relevant financial regulations and reporting requirements. Compliance algorithms help monitor and enforce adherence to these rules.

Quantitative hedge funds rely on a combination of quantitative research, data analysis, mathematical modeling, and algorithmic trading to gain a competitive edge in financial markets. The use of technology and automation allows these funds to execute complex strategies efficiently and manage risk effectively while seeking to deliver consistent returns to investors.

Chapter 10: Future Trends in Algorithmic Trading

Emerging Technologies and Trends

Algorithmic trading is a dynamic field that continues to evolve, driven by advancements in technology, changes in market structure, and shifts in investor behavior. Here are some emerging technologies and trends shaping the future of algorithmic trading:

1. Machine Learning and AI Advancements:

◈ Machine learning and artificial intelligence are expected to play an increasingly prominent role in algorithmic trading. Advanced ML models, including deep learning, reinforcement learning, and natural language processing, will be used for predictive modeling, pattern recognition, and risk management.

2. Quantum Computing:

◈ Quantum computing has the potential to revolutionize algorithmic trading by solving complex optimization problems and analyzing vast datasets at speeds that are currently unimaginable. As quantum computing technology matures, it may open up new avenues for trading strategies and risk assessment.

3. Big Data Analytics:

◈ The volume of data available for analysis continues to grow. Algorithmic traders will leverage big data analytics to gain insights from alternative data sources, including social media sentiment, satellite imagery, and IoT devices, to inform their trading decisions.

4. Blockchain and Distributed Ledger Technology:

◈ Blockchain and distributed ledger technology have the potential to enhance transparency, security, and settlement processes in financial markets. Algorithmic traders may explore opportunities in tokenized assets and decentralized finance (DeFi) markets.

5. High-Frequency Trading (HFT) Evolution:

◈ HFT strategies will continue to evolve, with a focus on optimizing speed, reducing latency, and incorporating advanced risk management techniques. The pursuit of microsecond and nanosecond trading speeds will persist.

6. Cryptocurrency and Digital Asset Trading:

◈ Algorithmic trading in the cryptocurrency and digital asset markets is expected to expand as these markets mature. Algorithms will be used for arbitrage, market making, and trading across various digital assets and exchanges.

7. Regulation and Compliance Technology:

◈ Regulatory technology (RegTech) solutions will become increasingly important for algorithmic traders to ensure compliance with evolving financial regulations. Algorithms will play a role in automating regulatory reporting and risk assessment.

8. Sustainability and ESG Integration:

◈ Algorithmic trading strategies will incorporate environmental, social, and governance (ESG) factors into decision-making. Sustainable and responsible investing strategies will gain prominence.

9. Robo-Advisors and Retail Algorithmic Trading:

◈ Robo-advisors and retail-focused algorithmic trading platforms will continue to grow in popularity. These platforms will offer algorithmic trading strategies to retail investors, making automated trading more accessible.

10. Market Microstructure Innovations: - Changes in market microstructure, such as the introduction of new order types and venues, will impact algorithmic trading. Algorithms will adapt to these evolving market dynamics.

11. Explainable AI and Model Interpretability: - As AI-driven algorithms become more prevalent, there will be an increased emphasis on making these models explainable and interpretable. Regulators and investors will demand transparency in algorithmic decision-making.

12. Cybersecurity and Data Privacy: - With the growing importance of data in algorithmic trading, cybersecurity and data privacy will be critical concerns. Traders will invest in robust cybersecurity measures to protect against cyber threats and data breaches.

13. Hybrid Models: - Hybrid models that combine human expertise with machine learning and automation will become more prevalent. These models harness the strengths of both humans and machines to make trading decisions.

14. Global Market Access: - Algorithmic traders will seek opportunities in emerging markets and regions with evolving financial infrastructure. Expanding global market access will require adaptive algorithms and market-specific strategies.

The future of algorithmic trading is marked by increasing complexity, technological innovation, and the integration of advanced analytical techniques. Traders and financial institutions that remain agile and embrace these emerging technologies and trends are likely to stay competitive in the rapidly evolving landscape of algorithmic trading.

Big Data and Artificial Intelligence (AI) play a crucial role in algorithmic trading by providing traders and financial institutions with the tools to analyze vast amounts of data, make informed decisions, and develop sophisticated trading strategies. Here's a closer look at the role of Big Data and AI in algorithmic trading:

1. Data Analysis and Processing:

◈ Big Data technologies enable the collection, storage, and processing of vast amounts of financial data from various sources, including historical price data, order book data, news feeds, and social media. AI algorithms can then analyze this data to identify patterns, correlations, and anomalies.

2. Predictive Modeling:

◈ AI, particularly machine learning, is used to build predictive models that forecast future price movements, volatility, and market trends. These models can be based on historical data, market sentiment analysis, and other factors, allowing traders to make data-driven decisions.

3. Pattern Recognition:

◈ Machine learning algorithms excel at recognizing complex patterns in financial data. Traders use AI to identify technical analysis patterns, candlestick patterns, and other signals that can inform trading strategies.

4. Sentiment Analysis:

◈ Natural language processing (NLP) and sentiment analysis techniques are used to assess news articles, social media posts, and other textual data for market sentiment. AI algorithms can gauge whether news sentiment is bullish, bearish, or neutral and incorporate this information into trading decisions.

5. Portfolio Optimization:

◈ AI-driven portfolio optimization algorithms help traders construct portfolios that balance risk and return. These algorithms consider factors like asset correlations, risk tolerance, and return expectations to create diversified and well-balanced portfolios.

6. Risk Management:

◈ AI is integral to risk management in algorithmic trading. Machine learning models can assess portfolio risk, monitor exposure to different asset classes, and recommend hedging strategies to mitigate risk.

7. High-Frequency Trading (HFT):

◈ In HFT, AI is used to develop ultra-fast trading algorithms that make split-second decisions. These algorithms rely on AI-driven predictive models and statistical arbitrage techniques to capture small price discrepancies.

8. Regulatory Compliance:

◈ AI algorithms help automate regulatory compliance processes by monitoring trading activities for potential violations and generating required reports. This ensures that trading operations adhere to evolving financial regulations.

9. Market Microstructure Analysis:

◈ AI-driven algorithms analyze market microstructure data to gain insights into order flow, liquidity patterns, and market impact. This information is used to optimize execution strategies.

10. Algorithmic Trading Strategy Development: - AI-powered platforms and tools assist traders in developing, backtesting, and refining algorithmic trading strategies. These platforms use machine learning to adapt and improve strategies based on changing market conditions.

11. Real-Time Decision-Making: - AI algorithms can make real-time trading decisions based on incoming data feeds, news events, and market conditions. These algorithms can execute orders, manage positions, and adapt strategies within milliseconds.

12. Adaptive Strategies: - AI-driven algorithms are adaptive and can adjust trading strategies in response to changing market dynamics. They continuously learn and adapt to evolving market conditions.

13. Alternative Data Integration: - Big Data and AI enable the integration of alternative data sources, such as satellite imagery, social media sentiment, and economic indicators, into trading strategies. These non-traditional data sources provide additional insights into market trends and opportunities.

The combination of Big Data and AI empowers algorithmic traders to make data-driven decisions, enhance strategy development and execution, and manage risk more effectively. As these technologies continue to advance, algorithmic trading strategies are becoming increasingly sophisticated and capable of handling complex financial markets.

Algorithmic trading in a decentralized world refers to the application of automated trading strategies in markets and ecosystems built on decentralized technologies, such as blockchain, decentralized finance (DeFi), and cryptocurrencies. Here's an overview of algorithmic trading in this context:

1. Decentralized Exchanges (DEXs):

◈ Decentralized exchanges, which operate on blockchain platforms like Ethereum, allow users to trade cryptocurrencies directly without the need for intermediaries. Algorithmic trading on DEXs involves the use of smart contracts to automate order execution, liquidity provision, and arbitrage strategies.

2. Automated Market Makers (AMMs):

◈ AMMs are smart contract-based algorithms that provide liquidity to decentralized exchanges. Algorithmic traders can participate in AMM pools to earn fees and optimize their positions. Popular AMMs include Uniswap and SushiSwap.

3. DeFi Liquidity Provision:

◈ Algorithmic trading strategies are used to provide liquidity to DeFi protocols. Traders can automate the process of lending assets on decentralized lending platforms like Compound or participating in yield farming to earn rewards.

4. Flash Loans and Arbitrage:

◈ Flash loans, enabled by DeFi protocols, allow traders to borrow large sums of assets without collateral as long as they return the borrowed amount within a single transaction block. Traders use flash loans for arbitrage opportunities across various DeFi platforms.

5. Smart Order Routing (SOR) on DeFi:

◈ In a decentralized world, SOR algorithms optimize the routing of trades across multiple decentralized exchanges and liquidity pools to achieve the best execution for users. These algorithms consider factors like gas fees, liquidity depth, and slippage.

6. Decentralized Derivatives Markets:

◈ Decentralized derivatives platforms, such as Synthetix and dYdX, enable algorithmic trading of synthetic assets, futures, and options without relying on centralized intermediaries. Traders can automate strategies involving derivatives.

7. Algorithmic Stablecoin Management:

◈ Algorithmic stablecoins like DAI rely on algorithms to maintain their peg to a stable asset (e.g., the U.S. dollar). Traders can participate in algorithmic stablecoin systems to earn rewards by managing collateral and debt positions.

8. Automated Yield Optimization:

◈ DeFi yield aggregators and protocols like Yearn Finance use algorithms to automate the optimization of yield generation by moving funds between different DeFi platforms. These algorithms seek the highest yield with minimal risk.

9. DeFi Risk Management:

◈ Algorithmic risk management tools are used in DeFi to assess the risk associated with various lending, borrowing, and liquidity provision strategies. These tools can help traders make informed decisions and protect their assets.

10. Decentralized Oracles: - Decentralized oracles, such as Chainlink, provide trusted external data to smart contracts. Algorithmic trading strategies in decentralized markets may rely on these oracles to access real-world data for decision-making.

11. Governance Participation: - DeFi platforms often involve governance tokens that allow users to participate in decision-making. Algorithms can be used to analyze governance proposals and vote on behalf of token holders.

12. Regulatory Considerations: - Algorithmic trading in decentralized ecosystems may face evolving regulatory challenges, as the regulatory framework for DeFi and cryptocurrencies continues to develop globally.

Algorithmic trading in a decentralized world offers increased accessibility, transparency, and programmability compared to traditional financial markets. However, it also presents unique challenges related to smart contract vulnerabilities, security, and regulatory compliance. Traders and developers in the DeFi space need to stay informed about the rapidly evolving landscape and adopt best practices for security and risk management.

Preparing for the future of algorithmic trading requires a combination of staying up-to-date with emerging trends and technologies, adapting to changing market conditions, and maintaining a commitment to risk management and compliance. Here are steps and considerations for preparing for the future of algorithmic trading:

1. Stay Informed:

◈ Continuously educate yourself and your team about the latest developments in algorithmic trading, including emerging technologies, market structure changes, and regulatory updates.

2. Embrace Technology:

◈ Invest in state-of-the-art technology infrastructure to ensure low latency, reliable connectivity, and high processing power. Consider the adoption of emerging technologies like quantum computing and advanced machine learning models.

3. Data Management:

◈ Develop robust data management processes to handle the growing volume of data in algorithmic trading. Consider the use of big data analytics and data cleansing techniques.

4. Advanced Analytics:

◈ Embrace advanced analytics, including machine learning and artificial intelligence, to gain insights from data, develop predictive models, and enhance trading strategies.

5. Regulatory Compliance:

◈ Keep abreast of evolving regulatory requirements for algorithmic trading. Implement compliance measures, such as pre-trade risk checks and reporting systems, to adhere to regulatory standards.

6. Risk Management:

◈ Prioritize risk management by continuously monitoring and assessing your trading strategies and portfolios. Develop robust risk models and stress tests to mitigate potential losses.

7. Cybersecurity:

◈ Strengthen cybersecurity measures to protect trading systems and sensitive data. Regularly audit and update security protocols to defend against cyber threats.

8. Talent and Skill Development:

◈ Hire and train professionals with expertise in algorithmic trading, data science, and technology. Encourage ongoing skill development to keep your team's knowledge current.

9. Diversification:

◈ Consider diversifying your trading strategies and asset classes to adapt to changing market conditions and reduce risk.

10. Ethical Considerations: - Ensure ethical and responsible use of algorithmic trading. Be aware of ethical concerns related to high-frequency trading and the impact on market fairness.

11. Market Microstructure Knowledge: - Deepen your understanding of market microstructure, including order types, execution algorithms, and liquidity dynamics. This knowledge is essential for optimizing execution strategies.

12. Algorithm Testing and Validation: - Establish rigorous testing and validation procedures for algorithms before deploying them in live trading. Backtesting and simulation are critical steps in algorithm development.

13. Regulatory Liaison: - Maintain open communication with regulatory authorities to stay informed about regulatory changes and to address any concerns or inquiries promptly.

14. Environmental and Social Responsibility: - Consider the environmental and social impact of algorithmic trading activities. Strive to align trading strategies with sustainability and ethical standards.

15. Adaptive Strategies: - Develop algorithms that can adapt to changing market conditions and incorporate machine learning models that can self-adjust based on evolving data patterns.

16. Scenario Planning: - Develop scenario-based strategies and contingency plans for unexpected events, such as market crashes or system failures.

17. Collaborate with Industry: - Collaborate with industry peers, technology providers, and academic institutions to share knowledge and best practices in algorithmic trading.

Preparing for the future of algorithmic trading requires a proactive and flexible approach. By staying informed, embracing technology, prioritizing risk management, and maintaining compliance, you can position yourself to navigate the evolving landscape of algorithmic trading successfully.

In conclusion, algorithmic trading has come a long way since its inception, evolving from simple rule-based strategies to complex, data-driven systems that harness the power of artificial intelligence and big data. The future promises even greater advancements in technology, market structure, and trading strategies.

As we venture into this exciting future, staying informed, embracing innovation, and maintaining a commitment to responsible and ethical trading practices will be the keys to success. Whether you are a quantitative hedge fund, a high-frequency trader, a retail investor, or a developer in the decentralized finance space, the world of algorithmic trading offers opportunities for growth, innovation, and profitability.

By continually adapting to change, investing in cutting-edge technology, and adhering to the highest standards of risk management and compliance, you can prepare yourself for the challenges and opportunities that lie ahead in the ever-evolving world of algorithmic trading.

So, as we look to the horizon of algorithmic trading, let us remember that the future is a landscape of limitless possibilities, where knowledge, innovation, and adaptability will lead us to new heights of success in the dynamic world of finance.

Also by Alex Thompson

Alex on Finance

Financial Freedom Roadmap - Achieving Early Retirement through the FIRE Movement
The Art of Strategic Innovation
Beyond Cash - The Evolution of Digital Payment Systems and the Future of Money
Preserving Wealth in Inflationary Times - Strategies for Protecting Your Financial Future

Standalone

Side Hustle Success: Unlocking Your Entrepreneurial Potential
Side Hustle Success: The Ultimate Guide to Passive and Financial Freedom
Mastering the Markets: Advanced Trading Strategies for Success and Ethical Trading Practices
Financial Fortitude
Mastering the Art of Upselling
The Financial Bullet Blueprint
Investing Demystified: A Beginner's Guide to Building Wealth in the Stock Market
Real Estate Riches: Building Wealth through Property Investment
How To Succeed as a Freelancer

Navigating Complex Waters: Advanced Strategies in Portfolio Management
Behavioral Finance and Investor Psychology
Leading with Empathy: Harnessing Emotional Intelligence for Effective Leadership
Financial Independence
Thriving Within Your Means: A Guide to Affordable Living
Algorithmic Trading: Navigating the Digital Frontier
Navigating Alternative Investments
Navigating the Behavioral Finance Landscape
Unlocking the Power of Derivatives
Mastering International Finance
Quantitative Finance and Risk Modeling
Sustainable and ESG Investing
Derivatives Dynamics: Navigating Risk and Innovation
Options Mastery: Navigating the Financial Frontier
Portfolio Mastery: Navigating the Financial Art and Science
Ethics in Hedge Funds: Navigating the Moral Compass of Finance
Structured Finance: Navigating Innovation, Sustainability and Ethics
Commodity Trading: Navigating Markets, Sustainability, and Innovation
Ethical Valuation: Navigating the Future of Startup Investments
Navigating Financial Risk: Strategies for a Dynamic World
Navigating the New Frontier: Understanding Market Microstructure in the Digital Age
Mastering Mergers and Acquisitions: Strategies, Successes and Lessons
Mastering Real Estate Investment: Strategies, Trends and Success Stories
Navigating Investor Behavior: Insights from Behavioral Finance
Private Equity Horizons: Navigating Opportunities and Shaping the Future
Algorithmic Trading: Navigating the Future of Finance

www.ingramcontent.com/pod-product-compliance
Lightning Source LLC
LaVergne TN
LVHW100326210926
848480LV00003B/1264
* 9 7 9 8 2 2 3 4 2 4 4 9 9 *